dedication

To Nonno Sabato and Nonna Maria Carmela whose faith, sacrifice, hard work, determination and love, during the hardest of times in Cannalonga, provided a better life for their family.

To Nonno Giovanni and Nonna Luigina whose vision, commitment, courage and sacrifice saw them leaving their familiar homeland in search of a better life for their family.

Mentre mai completamente capirò che vita era come per voi ... credilo quando dico che siete molto l'ispirazione per questo libro e l'ispirazione per la specie di vita Luisa e mi commetto alla costruzione per la nostra famiglia.

[Whilst I will never fully understand what life was like for you ... believe me when I say that you are very much the inspiration for this book and the inspiration for the sort of life Luisa and I are committed to building for our family.]

carmela antuoni sabato pizzolante carmela pizzolante (child) 1963

giovanni and luigina musto 1969

forewords

I was born in England, raised in New Zealand but have spent the majority of my years in Australia. If I had however been given a choice where I would have most like to have been born, I would probably go first of all for Paris (the natural habitat of terrine, Beaujolais and chic). Anywhere in Italy would be my clear second choice.

The importance of the family, the inventiveness, the frugality, the espresso, the joy of life, in short … the Italian way. Unfortunately where we are born is not something we get to have a say in. Yet if we are wise we can learn lessons from different cultures and apply them to our own world. Mark Pomery, in this wonderful book, allows us to saunter with him on his journey from uncultured Aussie to Italian aficionado.

The lessons are pervasive and persuasive because a whole country stands behind them. Their experience can be our instruction.

I think we all need to be a little more Italian and if nothing else this book will certainly improve the flavour of your ragu and chicken cacciatora.

Of course, if you really are Italian you won't go and buy this book you will borrow it from a friend or write to the local library to get it in. On second thoughts a quick peruse of the contents will convince that this is certainly the kind of volume that will prove to be as indispensable as a good bottle of olive oil … and slightly cheaper.

PHIL BAKER - SENIOR MINISTER
RIVERVIEW CHURCH, PERTH, WESTERN AUSTRALIA
BEST-SELLING AUTHOR OF SEVEN BOOKS INCLUDING *SECRETS OF SUPER ACHIEVERS* AND *A WISEHEART - THE FORGOTTEN FACTOR*

Mark Pomery has dished up a delicious book. It's fun and thought provoking. It does for the mind what a great meal does for the body; it leaves you with a feeling of being nourished and ready. 'What The Church Family Can Learn From The Italian Family' is an entertaining recipe. It's a zesty mixture of history, culture, social idiosyncrasies and Christian faith.

In a world of rapid technological advancement and sociological sophistication, we have found ourselves hungry for the simple things. And these simple things release the flavors that bring joy to life and relationships. Read this book. It will help you to put your finger on some missing ingredients in your journey.

Bravo, Mark Pomery. You can prepare a meal in the kitchen of my mind anytime!

WES BEAVIS - BEST-SELLING AUTHOR
BECOME THE PERSON YOU DREAM OF BEING & GIVE YOUR LIFE A SUCCESS MAKEOVER

endorsements

"*Every migrant will relate to the hilarious, yet insightful stories that Mark shares in this enjoyable book. Mark displays an amazing ability to bridge two contrasting worlds, and in the process, uncovers some powerful principles from the Italian world which if applied, will revolutionise the Church world as we know it.*"

ANDREW RANUCCI - SENIOR PASTOR
COAST COMMUNITY CHURCH, CENTRAL COAST, SYDNEY, AUSTRALIA

Jamie Oliver showed us how NOT to do it, offending Italians everywhere... How annoying as a European to be recommending instead an Aussie as your guide to all things Italian - if you want an insightful message, combined with timeless truths and served up with a liberal dash of humour, Mark Pomery is the Godfather!

ANTHONY DELANEY - SENIOR MINISTER
LIFE CHURCH, SURREY, ENGLAND.

How can anything so thought provoking, so relevant, be so funny? Mark Pomery has found a way to communicate with this book, providing strength for the spirit and delight for the senses!

TOM VILLALOBOS - SENIOR MINISTER
OAK VALLEY FAMILY CHURCH, CALIFORNIA, USA

WHAT THE CHURCH FAMILY
CAN LEARN FROM THE ITALIAN FAMILY

All enquiries regarding this publication and Mark Pomery's speaking engagements to be made to:

Mark Pomery
PO Box 524 Victoria Park Western Australia 6979
enquiries@markpomery.com   www.markpomery.com

Refer to the end of this book for more information concerning the author, Mark Pomery.

Printed in Australia by Hyde Park Press, Richmond, South Australia

ISBN 0 9775072 0 3

what the
CHURCH FAMILY
can learn from the
ITALIAN FAMILY

index

introduction

Introduzione

To adapt a line from the movie, 'My Big Fat Greek Wedding', (which could have quite easily been called My Big Fat Italian Wedding as it was eerie in its similarity to my wedding), "There are two types of people in the world ... Italians and those that wanna be Italian!" Now while I know this is not true of everyone, you will be hard pressed to convince the Italians otherwise.

On 3 January 1998 I married a beautiful girl named Luisa Pizzolante. Now although Luisa was born in Australia, with a name like that it's easy to guess that her parents are originally from Italy. .

After World War 2, when the Italians migrated to Australia en masse, a racial taunt was to call them 'Dings' or 'Wogs'. Most Australians were unaware that in response the pragmatic Italians would refer to them as 'Skips', after the colloquial name for kangaroos.

Since marrying into an Italian family I have discovered that over time the Italians take on us Skips has evolved further. They have developed a ranking system of various categories of 'Skips'.

The first and lowest level is the 'Basic Skip'. This is the person who has a very low-level understanding and appreciation of Italians. The Basic Skip thinks there is only one type of Italian pasta dish ... Spaghetti Bolognese; that parmesan cheese is grown in cardboard tubes, and that real pizza is made with ham and pineapple on top (what my mother-in-law refers to, with great disdain, as 'Fruit Salad')

The next category up from the 'Basic Skip' is the 'Wanna Be Italian'. This is someone who, whilst having no Italian blood loves all things Italian ... pasta, Chianti, Lamborghinis and so on. They have read 'Under The Tuscan Sun' and know where to buy Italian smallgoods.

Much to my surprise, in recent years I actually discovered there was another lesser-known category, a step up from a 'Wanna-Be Italian'. This category is the closest you can get to being Italian without actually being Italian. This category of person is known as an 'IBM' ... or, an 'Italian By Marriage'. Obviously I qualify for this category (and I have the T-Shirt to prove it!)

Now don't get the wrong impression that upon marrying Luisa I immediately soared to great heights in the estimation of my new family. Upon marriage you might get to stake your claim as an IBM but you still have to earn your stripes! Still, the pain is worth it.

So over the first several years of marriage I certainly didn't see this book coming. The lessons I have found myself learning over the years have been a progressive revelation. I have found myself at various times challenged, inspired, frustrated, enamoured, shocked, confused, and lost for words in admiration. God has used this journey, and continues to do so, in surprising ways to highlight things about the Italian family that I am consequently trying to apply to my walk as a Christian and to my part in my local Church.

In this book I want to draw some lessons from my experience of having married into this crazy family, and the unique Italian culture, that I believe have direct application to individual Christians and the Church as a whole.

My prayer is that, through reading this, you will join with me in exploring the wonder of the Italian family, and that God, as He continues to do for me, will impress things on your heart that will cause your relationship with your family to deepen, your walk with God to be enriched, and your part in your local Church to be more effective.

The Truth Is Stranger (And More Amazing) Than Fiction!

In countries like Australia, the US and Canada, where there are large numbers of Italian immigrants, people (me included) grew up with some stereotypes of the Italian immigrant culture.

I believed that they eat a lot of food. I believed that they all drive Monaros (a large, powerful, Australian-manufactured muscle car) with fluffy dice hanging from the rear view mirror. I believed that they do lots of talking. In fact I heard it said once that the three most effective methods of communication are the telephone, the television and to tell an Italian.

Since marrying into this family I have had the opportunity to find out first-hand that not only are these stereotypes actually true, but that the reality far surpasses the stereotypes.

The content and emphasis of this book have been drawn primarily from my observations of the Italians who first immigrated to Australia, as well as those who still live in smaller villages back in Italy, as they are very much the people who have inspired me in the things I write of.

At various times I have been tempted to apologise for the sweeping generalities I attribute to the Italians, yet I continue to meet Italians throughout the world who can relate directly to the stories I have told, and validate my stories

I have since had the privilege of meeting Italians in many countries of the world and they can all relate to the stories that have been my experience. Somehow, despite the fact these people or their parents grew up in different regions in Italy and migrated to different corners of the world, the Italian DNA is so strong it has been impregnated into unsuspecting corners of the globe.

So it is with great pride, incredible humility (yes, I know that sounds oxymoronic!), and eager anticipation, that I commit these things to paper in the hope that you too will be inspired and, in turn, the church of Jesus Christ will shine brighter than ever as a result of our applying these vital principles in increasing measure.

Italy ... The Land Flowing With Vino And Pasta!

Italy has exerted an influence in world affairs and culture very much disproportionate to its size and population, and has done so for hundreds of years. Very few nations and cultures have had such a far-reaching impact, particularly into Western society, as the Italians. It was the Italian post-war(s) diaspora that saw Italian culture go global and put us in touch with it. Their journeys resembled missionaries dispatched to spread the gospel in remote corners of the earth.

Many have fallen in love with the Italian ways of making food (there are an estimated 3500 Italian restaurants in Tokyo alone!), creating fashion, manufacturing glamorous cars, and so on.

I will be the first one to admit that I have been completely sucked into the vortex, fascinated with all things Italian. I didn't seek it, I don't really know how it happened ... it just kind of snuck up on me.

God has used many experiences and many people, during my years of marriage to Luisa and my subsequent immersion into the Italian and the Italian migrant culture, to reveal more of His character and to show me insights into what the Church can really become.

Before you get your knickers in a twist, accusing me of blasphemy and reminding me that God's picture of the Church is already contained in the Bible, I am simply saying that God has used many experiences as sort of modern-day parables to underscore truths about how He wants His Church to be and it's these that I want to share with you in this book.

Being Italian is a mindset as much as a culture and way of life. My goal in this book is to take a look behind the curtain as to what has, over the years, created the Italian mindset and, armed with those insights, my prayer is that we can achieve 'Italian-style' results in our spheres of influence ... our families, our Churches and our communities.

Just as there is much we can learn from the early Church as described in the book of Acts, I have personally experienced many things from the Italians that reinforce God's best plan for His Church.

God wants His Church to be a land flowing with milk and honey and I will endeavour to stir things up in you from lessons I have learned from the land flowing with vino and pasta!

So *SALUTE*' and read on!

lesson number one
Lezione Numero Uno

my house is your house
La Mia Casa e' La Tua Casa

1

Italians are known for their generosity and their hospitality. When I started dating Luisa I naively chose Easter Sunday to be my first Sunday lunch with her family. I'll set the scene ...

At the time I was a 'Basic Skip', having been raised on a nightly diet of 'meat-and-three-veg'. Add to this the fact I was, at that time, a starving bible college student, living in an apartment by myself. These two factors left me wide-open to the events that followed.

I am now the leading campaigner for the introduction of rules for dating an Italian, that need to include either a *'Don't Make Easter Sunday Lunch Your First Experience At The Italian Table'* or *'If You Are Stupid Enough To Make Easter Sunday Lunch Your First Experience At An Italian Table Your Italian Girlfriend Should Conduct A Thorough Briefing About What you Can Expect Over The Next Several Hours'.*

Prior to my arrival at her family's dining table Luisa didn't mention a thing.

I walked in and it seemed the table was *already* laden with what I concluded was enough food for three hundred guests. I'm convinced the Italian dining room is like Dr Who's Tardis - from the outside they look small but you walk in and they can comfortably cram forty people around a card table!

On the table was Luisa's Grandmother's *(Nonna's)* homemade wood-fired bread, sliced Italian sausage, six different types of cheeses, olives, prosciutto ... it struck me as the greatest spread of food I had ever seen for a lunch. I thought it was so fantastic that at the very second they issued the invitation, 'Marco, help yourself.' It was at this point that I lost complete touch with reality. I just started eating, figuring that if I ate fast enough my stomach would be full before my brain acknowledges the consumption (I'm told you have a 20-minute window before the brain is triggered) and I would save precious dollars by not having to eat dinner that night.

Ignorant as it sounds to me now, as a 'Basic Skip' I had not previously heard the term *antipasti* ... the amazing variety and quantity of food laid out on the table was only intended to precede the entrée! Then came a bowl of pasta - homemade lasagna - which I consumed without even looking up. They asked me if I wanted some more and despite the fact that I was already full after the *antipasti* I said, 'Yes!'

After three serves of lasagna, Luisa's mum, Josie, foisted the second round of pasta on me - spinach fettuccine with cream and mushrooms. It was at this juncture I had to loosen my belt. The fettuccine was so nice ... I had two bowls!

When a sumptuous fish concoction was then served I promptly ignored the words penned by Shakespeare, "Never, never, never, never, never! Pray you, undo this button."[1] I discreetly shifted my napkin so I could undo the top button of my jeans without anyone noticing. Seemingly a few short minutes later chicken was served - pop goes button number two!

The room had started spinning, my swelling of my stomach had pushed me eight inches away from the table, I had already loosened two buttons. The only choice facing me at that time was whether to take my pants off altogether or excuse myself from the table and convalesce on the couch. As this was my first meal with the family I didn't think removing my pants was the sort of first impression I wanted to make.

That was Sunday lunch. I did not consume another morsel of food until Tuesday night!

Only a few months later I witnessed what I considered at the time to be one of the most scandalous, rude and selfish things I had ever had the misfortune of seeing.

I was at Luisa's family's house early on a Saturday afternoon. We had finished a nice, simple lunch of pasta and salad and were relaxing in the lounge room when out of the blue one of Luisa's cousins, Sabby, popped in. Josie offered him something to eat, of which he accepted.

Josie re-heated a bowl of pasta in the microwave (re-heating and defrosting are the only two approved uses for a microwave to the Italians!), Sabby ate it, and then promptly left.

Now, as an eyewitness to this short series of events, let me record the crime and the associated charges as I saw it at the time through my pre-IBM eyes ...

Crime #1: Sabby dropped in unannounced! In my upbringing this would be unheard of. He should have called up several days in advance to allow time to clean the house and possibly prepare some food. He should have also had a good reason for coming over ... 'I was just driving by so I thought I would say "Hi!"' simply isn't good enough!

Crime #2: Sabby accepted food on the first offer! In my upbringing when you are offered food it is polite to say 'No' on two occasions (and say, "Oh, just a cup of tea will be fine"), before saying 'Yes' to the third offer.

Crime #3: Sabby immediately sat at the table! According to my upbringing he should have first joined us in the lounge room for at least twenty minutes and engaged in idle preliminary conversation before graduating to the table.

Crime #4: Sabby ate the food in the space of only a few minutes and then left! In my upbringing this shows a complete lack of respect. He should have finished the food, returned to the lounge room (which I would like to remind you he did not enter in the first place!) and engaged in another twenty minutes (minimum) of idle pre-departure conversation. This shows gratitude.

Sabby was guilty of at least these four crimes as I saw it. But that's just the point. I was witnessing the situation through my 'Skip' eyes. I am in no way putting down my upbringing (my English-born Assistant, Regan, also related entirely to the above four points) but am merely making the point that the Italian family is different in their expectations.

You see, Sabby wasn't viewed as a visitor *or* a guest ... he is family. That house was as much his house as the one he actually lived in with his own parents. And that food was as much his food as the food at his own house.

When we go to see Luisa's Grandparents I am further reminded that they see everything they have as being ours as well.

One time, my friend Phil was having a few people over to his house for dinner and I took on the task of providing some of the food and doing some of the cooking.

On the way to Phil's house Luisa and I thought we would pick up some supplies - not from the supermarket but from Luisa's grandparents - some homemade tomato sauce for the pasta, homemade wood fired pizza ... just brilliant food! When we got there they asked us to sit down. Naturally we had allocated thirty minutes before we had to leave for Phil's to allow us to have a chat with them.

They instinctively asked if we wanted to have dinner, however we informed them we were going out for dinner and reminded them that this was why we were picking up the food in the first place.

Note - When Italians ask if you want to have dinner it is a rhetorical question at best, though in reality it is more a statement of what you are going to do next whether you want to or not!

In the blink of an eye out came bread, cheese, sausage, *vino* (must have a *vino* with the sausage, no *vino*, no sausage!). We reminded them, 'But we are going to dinner now.' To which the reflexive response from Luisa's Grandfather *(Nonno)* came, 'Yeah I know ... you eat!'

It was after consuming these snacks that I learnt the Italian expression: *per il viaggio* - for the trip. As we got up to leave to go to Phil's, Luisa's grandparents both momentarily disappeared. Moments later her Grandfather returned with a bottle of *vino*, which he insisted I take and assured me it was the best I would ever have, and Luisa's Grandmother re-emerged with two shopping bags of food items, to be added to the things we had gone there to pick up in the first instance ... all *per il viaggio!*

We duly pointed out to them that they lived less than five minutes from Phil's house, hence we would not really need anything *per il viaggio*. A loaf of wood-fired bread, an Italian sausage, *finnocchio* biscuits (sometimes called *Taralli* - try them with some cheese ... you won't be disappointed!) and a bottle of wine for a three-minute *viaggio!*

But, of course, this was not the point to them. The point was they wanted us to take something from their house (and indeed their heart) back to our house. Italians are committed to your leaving their house with more than when you came.

I turned up to Phil's house with no more room for food in my stomach! I cooked dinner and stood by idly while everyone else ate!

Luisa's Grandfather, Giovanni, was always telling us, 'You come over any time.' The interesting subtlety is that it was never motivated by his needs but rather by his desire to share what he had with us at every opportunity.

Why The Italians Are Generous

Perche Gli Italiani Sono Generosi

Today, Luisa's parents, Carmine and Josie, lead a reasonably normal suburban life in a three-bedroom house in a suburb of Perth, Western Australia. However, life for them was not always this comfortable.

In 2004, Luisa and I had the great privilege of going to Italy and spending time with the family members who still live in the region her parents came from, the region of Campania. Carmine's village is called Cannalonga and Josie's village, only four villages away (about eight kilometres), is called Pattano. On a world scale, both these villages are merely dots of villages.

Josie came to Australia with her parents when she was only six years old. Carmine migrated to Australia when he was seventeen. They met and married here in Perth - quite a coincidence that their villages are so close.

After the Second World War Italy was devastated economically. Carmine's family couldn't afford to live and own a house in Cannalonga so the council allowed them to live in a hut on the other side of the neighbouring mountain, *Montagna Drascata*.

Their hut was only about ten metres by six metres. Nine people lived in that hut - Carmine's Dad and Mum, along with his five brothers, one sister and himself.

The land in that area is bleak, infertile, extremely rocky and virtually impossible to work, yet they were forced by circumstances to make a living out of farming it. Sharecropping with other families aided their survival, yet also rapidly exhausted what few nutrients were in the land.

When Carmine was five years old, his 'job' was to take excess produce to sell in Cannalonga and return with things the family needed. To do this required him to walk with a donkey over the mountain to Cannalonga - it was a three-hour-each-way walk. A pretty good effort at any age ... let alone five!

The kids had one pair of shoes between them. Whoever got up first got the shoes for the day.

I will never forget when we got back from Italy we were gathered with the family around the dining table, going through the 'holiday snaps' as you do. When Carmine first laid his eyes on the photo of his family's old hut it was like time stood still. I can't pretend to know what was going on his heart when he saw this. Tears welled up in his eyes and the moment rendered him speechless.

They were eventually able to afford to move into to Cannalonga, though up to that point survival had been a daily challenge. On some days his Mum, with her kids trailing behind her, would have to beg for wheat to be able to make enough bread for that day to feed her kids.

This was only just over fifty years ago and I am thankful that today they actually haven't forgotten what life was about back then, because this has formed the basis for the great lessons we can learn from them.

1. *Italiani* Have Enormous Gratitude

They are grateful they are still alive. They are grateful that, when their Mum begged for some wheat, someone actually gave them

Pallano 13.12.1967
con morto a fetto
alle mio caro marito
ti farmi sapu a ti fano
piacere come diamo di
salute bacci dai tuo proto
dale tua cara moglie
Caro caro buone feste

Josephine
Luigina Amato

some wheat. They are grateful that, when they migrated, their new country gave them an opportunity for a brand new start.

Luisa's Grandmother's favourite expression is, "Thanks be for the God!" She is grateful that God was with them through the hardest of times and has kept them safe and helped them with their brand new start.

When Jesus first sent the disciples out for public ministry He reminded them why they needed to be generous, 'Freely you have received, freely give.'[2] From Jesus' perspective it was to be a natural, reflexive response ... highly pragmatic. The stuff that Jesus had done for them, given them and shown them, was never intended to be kept within a closed circle. The fact they had received so freely from Jesus was the basis for and the motivation for now going out and giving it away.

The Italians have a paradigm of generosity that goes beyond what we 'Skips' understand it to be. For 'Skips', generosity could be defined, at best, as being, "If you ask me for something that I have I will give it to you."

The Italian version of generosity transcends this ... they are willing to pour their lives out to you. They define it more like, 'Whatever we have is yours to begin with, there is no need to ask. La mia casa e' la tua casa!'

On the first day that Luisa and I were in Cannalonga in 2004, having met the various family members for the first time, we were in her Auntie Giovannina's kitchen and I noticed a bowl of fresh fruit on the bench. I felt like eating one of the mandarins and I turned to Luisa's Auntie Giovannina in my less-than-impeccable Italian and asked her if I could have a mandarin.

I will never forget the look on her face ... it was one of puzzled bewilderment. It seems she didn't understand what I had asked her. I thought the reason she didn't understand the question was because of my poor Italian grammar but Luisa promptly pointed out that she didn't understand the question because essentially nobody had ever asked it before ... it didn't make any sense to her. She just looked at me and said, 'Marco, *la mia casa e' la tua casa!*', which was her way of saying, 'There is no need to ask me permission to have anything ever again ... everything I have is yours already!'

2. *Italiani* Know There Is Always More

Paul wrote to the Church in Philippi,

> *"I rejoice greatly in the Lord that at last you have renewed your concern for me. Indeed you have been concerned but you have had no opportunity to show it. I am not saying this because I am in need for I have learned to be content whatever the circumstances. I know what it is to be in need and I know what is to have plenty. I have learned the secret to be content in any situation whether well fed or hungry, whether living in plenty or in want. I can do everything in Him who gives me strength."[3]*

Italians have lived through long periods where they have literally had nothing and from the ground to the hand to the mouth was a way of life. They know what is like to have nothing, and years on, as a result of the many great qualities the hardships brought out in them, what it is like to have plenty. Most of them have a trust in God and they know they can do everything through Him who gives them strength.

If Italians give something away, they simply keep working hard, keep being resourceful, keep trusting God, keep working together as a family and as a community, and there will always be more.

Application
Applicazione

An old Italian proverb says, *"Tante volte al pozzo va la secchia ch'ella vi lascia il manico o l'orecchia."* ("A pitcher/jug that goes to the well often is likely to get broken"). Life is lived better when we are more about what we can give out than what we can draw in.

The essence of *per il viaggio* is that you don't leave an Italian's house empty handed. As I said, a hallmark of their generosity is they are committed to ensure you leave their houses with more than you came.

We can too easily live over-protective lives, rapaciously clinging to what is ours, justifying our self-centred position with sentiments like, 'I worked hard to get it and I ain't giving it up easily.' However this is not the best way to live and it is not the way God intended. For Christians generosity should be a natural response to everything God has given and continues to give to us. It should be reflexive, a way of life ... as natural to us as breathing. We were spiritually dead without God and God has rescued us, saved us, given us everything ... what other response could be more appropriate than complete and unqualified gratitude and sharing that gratitude with others. Freely we have received so we should freely give.

However it's often very easy for us to fall into the delusion that somehow *we* deserve the credit for our relationship with God and our blessings in life. 'I have been praying and reading my Bible for one hour each day for ten years therefore I have a great relationship with God!' Whilst that may be true, your time spent with God and in His Word should build on your relationship; you can take no credit for being able to start the relationship in the first place.

Some even protest at that point, 'It was me who responded to the altar call that day ... it was me who prayed the sinner's prayer.' Yes, but never forget it was God who first sent His Son ... it was Jesus who died on the cross for you ... and it was God who caused Him to rise from the dead. You did not do any of that ... and that is the foundation of our gratitude.

Paul said it this way

> "Brothers, think of what you were when you were called. Not many of you were wise by human standards; not many were influential; not many were of noble birth. But God chose the foolish things of the world to shame the wise; God chose the weak things of the world to shame the strong. He chose the lowly things of this world and the despised things - and the things that are not - to nullify the things that are, so that no one may boast before him. It is because of Him that you are in Christ Jesus, who has become for us wisdom from God - that is, our righteousness, holiness and redemption. Therefore, as it is written: "Let him who boasts boast in the Lord."
> (1 Cor 1:26-30 NIV)

At the time of writing Luisa have just returned from four weeks in Italy ... one week of ministry and three weeks of eating! We spent part of the three weeks in Cannalonga, where a strange phenomenon developed. I discovered after a couple of days that a queue had formed of family members who were wanting to have us come to their house for a meal - uncles, aunties, cousins, second cousins, third cousins, second cousins of third cousins, and on it went.

The only way we were even going to get close to fitting in all the requests was to do an average of four to five meals a day. After two weeks I found I had lost my taste for Italian food ... after three weeks I had lost the will to live! (Fortunately, as a result of an extremely punishing jogging regime, I only put on two kilograms).

Now the fact that we were family is one reason so many people wanted to host and feed us, but I had never experienced it to this extent before and went on a quest to find out why our stocks had risen so rapidly. I soon discovered it was because the word had spread that I LOVE their food. I mean what's not to like? Everything is home grown, home made or home shot!

But it wasn't just the fact that I loved their food, it was the fact that after every second mouthful I told them I loved the food. It was quite an accomplishment, chewing and swallowing, as the smile on my face stretched my mouth from ear to ear. But I couldn't help but effusively compliment them ... their food was delicious, every single family in every single household at every single meal.

So my reputation for not only enjoying it but for expressing my enjoyment, of effectively honouring their culture, history and hard work, caused them to want to pour out more on me.

Those of you who are parents know this principle very well. When your children thank you for who are and for what you do, your reflexive response is to pour out more blessing on them. As they honour you, you want to bless them.

Then it comes as no surprise to find this timeless principle in scripture, where God the Father acts in exactly the same way. In Malachi Chapter 3 God challenges His people to honour Him with their lives, their material possessions and their finances, and promises that His reflexive response will be to 'throw open the floodgates of heaven and pour out so much blessing that you will not have room enough for it.'[4]

Just as our Italian relatives' reflexive response to my honouring of them was to pour out so much food that my stomach could not contain it, so it is with God when we are honouring and generous towards Him.

There is a proverb that says, 'Where there is no vision, the people perish.'⁵ The Spanish version of the Bible literally translates this as, "Where there is no vision, the people run wild like horses." This proverb can be applied to many areas of our life, including the world of generosity.

Luisa and I have a vision to give away obscene (in the nicest possible use of the word) amounts of money into the Kingdom of God over our lifetime. Not to win some competition, as our giving is done in secret, but because our lives have been and continue to be changed by being part of a Bible-believing local Church and we want to see millions more people right across the world experience the same transforming power of God in their lives.

To this end we begin every year by setting 'giving goals', before we set goals for how much we want to pay off our mortgage, how much we want to save, how much we want to invest. This is one way we put God first in our finances, by making our giving the first 'big rock' we put in our priorities for the year.

Then we strive to ensure that our financial management lines up to allow those goals to become a reality. We don't allow our money 'to run wild like horses', we don't 'cast off restraint' when it comes to the money that passes through our hands. We try to play good 'offense', investing wisely, looking to increase our value in our workplace, to position ourselves for promotion and increase. We also try to play good 'defense', not wasting money on frivolous items and impulse purchases, and keeping wastage to a minimum (see some of the 'Assorted Frugality Tips From The Italian Immigrants' at the end of the chapter on 'Resourcefulness').

In my experience and observations too many opportunities are wasted and too much money is wasted by Christians who 'run wild like horses' when it comes to the management of their money and, as a result, they are not able to maximize their generosity to the extent that God would want them to.

Our houses need to be other people's houses, open to family and friends in the good times and bad.

Our hearts need to be open to others, in good times and in bad. We need to rejoice with those who rejoice and weep with those who weep. Unfortunately, too many of us lack generosity in our hearts and we sometimes rejoice for those who weep and weep for those who rejoice.

The writer of the Book of Proverbs reminds us that 'The world of the generous gets larger and larger; the world of the stingy gets smaller and smaller.'[6] We were at Luisa's cousin's son's (got that?!), Aniello's, first birthday party recently and, while we were sitting at the table with some of her cousins, I kept hearing them say, 'Another "New Addition" ... another "New Addition".'

Not fully understanding the point they were making, I asked for an explanation. The reality is the 'blood' members of their family are always meeting more people, always inviting them into their homes and lives ... it doesn't matter who they are, who met them, everyone is permitted to bring their 'new friends' along to family gatherings - you don't even need to phone ahead to book an extra place, they will always find room in their homes and in their hearts for more people. Hence the running joke at family gatherings - the cousins looking around to see who is a 'New Addition' since the last gathering.

Their world grows larger and larger.

Our Churches need to be open to everyone, both to people within our family and to people not yet within our family.

Jesus said, "Now that I've put you there on a hilltop, on a light stand--shine! Keep open house; be generous with your lives. By opening up to others, you'll prompt people to open up with God, this generous Father in heaven."[7]

Instead of closed, inward focused Churches we need to communicate to unchurched people, 'Our Church is your Church. Everything that is here, all the services, all the people, all the love, it's for you. You don't have to ask to have it ... it's yours already. The reason we give money through our Church is to reach out to you. The reason we hold small groups in our homes is so you can come and connect as part of the family.'

The early church embraced this spirit. 'All the believers were one in heart and mind. No one claimed that any of his possessions was his own, but they shared everything they had.'[8] As new people came into their midst they were embraced and accessed everything life within a true biblical community can offer.

If we really believe that God is our provider, I mean *really* believe that GOD IS OUR PROVIDER, we ought not to be protective of anything in our lives. We should live with the confidence that we can give it away and God will provide for us. In fact the Bible says not only *does* He give back to us but also that He *multiplies* our giving ... He gives us more than we have given out.

For the people in our circle, *La mia casa* e' *la tua casa* ... my house is your house. For the people who don't yet know Christ in our world's, *La mia chiesa* e' *la tua chiesa* ... my Church is your Church. Whatever is here already you just come in and grab a hold of it for yourself.

lesson number two
Lezione Numero Due

the italians are passionate
Gli Italiani Sono Appassionati

2

*"When shall we live, if not now?" Lucius Annaeus Seneca
(c.4 BC - 65 AD)*

I don't think anyone who knows Italians needs reminding that Italians are passionate. The fact that performers such as the Three Tenors and Andrea Bocelli are popular in English-speaking countries, even though those listening don't understand a word of what is being sung, is a testament to their ability to move us with their passion.

Italian grandfathers pride themselves on knowing everything and always being right. It is a futile exercise getting into an argument with them at any time, as they will overpower you with volume, passion and conviction, no matter how misplaced their theories may or may not be. Logic and reason are optional extras that are secondary inclusions behind the passion of their convictions.

My observation is that you have not really fully experienced the evening news until you have sat next to an Italian grandfather who is watching the evening news. Luisa's grandfather, Giovanni, will get you a free, 'infallible', loud, 'expert', running commentary. I have to constantly remind him that I am watching the same news program he is and therefore an explanation of what is happening is unnecessary ... words that fall on deaf ears! It's not the story they feel is the most important issue, rather it's their opinion on the story that matters.

Giovanni will lean across and say, 'Marco, listen! I wanna explanation some-a-thing! You let me be the Prime Minister for just-a five minutes and I will fix-a everything!' (And this is coming from a man who comes from a country where their Prime Ministers tend to last only five minutes anyway?!)

The passion of Italian men does not limit itself to current affairs. In fact it peaks when it comes to soccer. The English cricket side may have the 'Barmy Army', the Indian cricket side the 'Swami Army' but Italian soccer teams have, what I call, the 'Salami Army', of which my father-in-law is an avid participant. And the support of the Italian national team, the 'Azzuri', is where the 'Passion-o-meter' goes off the charts!

You have never fully experienced a televised game of soccer until you have sat in the lounge room of an Italian during a World Cup Final where Italy is playing.

Carmine, along with his family, stayed up into the early hours of the morning, gathered in the family lounge room to watch the live telecast of the now famous 1994 World Cup Final, Italy versus Brazil.

Scores were level at the end of the game so it went into extra time. At the end of extra time scores were still level so the game came down to a penalty shoot-out. In a penalty shoot-out each team picks it's five best strikers to go kick-for-kick, with one penalty shot per person, in order to decide the result of the game.

Now I admit this would have been something of an emotional roller coaster for any soccer fan but to Carmine it was more like Mt Vesuvius threatening to destroy Pompeii all over again.

The game came down to the last penalty of the match, where Italy's hero, Roberto Baggio, was to take the deciding shot. Baggio lined up with the likelihood of his scoring considered a fait accompli ... and pushed the penalty over the cross bar ... Brazil wins the 1994 World Cup.

A split second later, and I mean a split second later, Luisa's family, who were still all sitting in the lounge room, looked across to the couch where Carmine had been sitting, only to realise he was no longer sitting there.

The fact that less than a second had transpired since Baggio's boot had made contact with the ball left them momentarily puzzled as to Carmine's whereabouts ... until they looked on the floor. He had passed out unconscious and slipped off the couch!

Italians, particularly the immigrants and those in the villages in Italy, have extreme levels of loyalty towards not only Italy in general, but also the region they come from. This parochialism is referred to as *campanilismo*.

The lack of objectivity rendered by *campanilismo* causes the Italians to view everything through region-coloured glasses. Luisa's family is from the Campania region of Italy, and their village about one-and-a-half hours south of the famous city of Pompeii. Many years ago Carmine entered the house at the end of a workday, having had the radio on in his car. The last song he heard before he got out of the car was Otis Redding's classic, 'Sitting On The Dock Of The Bay'. Carmine walked into the house and proudly declared, "That's a good song that one, 'Talking To The Doctor In Pompeii'!"

I know, it's hard to even begin to think how an Italian immigrant who had been living in Australia, and thus speaking English, for over ten years, could draw such a long bow and get the words of the song so mixed up, but such is the passion that comes from *campanilismo*.

Campanilismo Warning: When an Italian tells you the wine he makes is the best ... don't argue. When an Italian tells you the method for *limoncello* (or cheese, or sauce, or bread, or meatballs, or whatever) their family has made for generations is the best ... just nod in agreement. Even if you recall having had better from someone or somewhere else, don't admit to it. Realise there is no objectivity in their bold and definitive declaration ... it's all about passion, it's all about *campanilismo*.

Why The Italians Are Passionate

Perche Gli Italiani Sono Appassionati

I have to say, this aspect of the Italian way of life, along with it's close cousin, expressiveness, is one I have struggled with the most, as far as working out the 'why?'

Carmine simply said Italians are passionate because Latin people in general - Spanish, Mexicans, and so on - are passionate. That Italian passion is somehow a genetic quality ... passed down from generation to generation.

Well, I am afraid that doesn't give me too much insight as to the background ... perhaps this is just one of the those things that 'is' and we, best leave it at that and shift our focus instead on the example it lays before us.

Application

Applicazione

Whilst it's fine to be passionate about the current events being played out on the evening news, and it's okay to be passionate about soccer (especially the World Cup!), I think if anything has reason to evoke passion it is the Church of Jesus Christ. In fact the word 'fan' comes directly from the Latin *fanaticus*, which means 'worshipper at a temple'.

The creators of the English language agreed on another front. They felt the best word to describe someone who is welling up with positive emotional energy should be synonymous with those who have a relationship with God, hence the word enthusiasm, which means 'en-theos' ... In God.

One of Australia's leading commentators and self-professed atheist, Phillip Adams, said to a group of pastors at a conference we hosted several years ago, 'For Christians to believe what they say they believe and not to be passionate about it must be the highest form of blasphemy.'

If Christ really did rise from the dead, and if accepting Him as our personal Lord and Saviour assures us of abundant life here on earth and eternal life thereafter, then there should be nothing we are more excited about and nothing for which we are more committed to demonstrating our passion.

The German philosopher Nietzsche said, 'If the Christians expect me to believe in their Redeemer they have got to look a lot more redeemed!' There are times of sorrow and sadness, of course, but Christians ought frequently to exude a sense of joy because they have something to be joyful about.

I have been to churches that were so lacking passion that I lost the will to live half way through the service. And I've sat through sermons where I have found myself contemplating the premature death of the preacher after five minutes!

The joke is told of one boy who walked into a Church beside his mother and continued talking to her in his normal volume as they passed through the doors and into the Church. His mother was horrified and whispered in a firm tone, 'Sshh ... keep you voice down, this is God's house.' To which the little boy responded, 'Well, if I was God I'd move!'

By passion I am not talking about hype and fabricated excitement but rather an internal, unstoppable wellspring of joy, conviction, and commitment to living out our faith in a manner that non-Christians find compelling. There should be an unmistakable difference in us and in how we live our lives.

Our passion for God, for the things of God, for the family of God and for the House of God should be a natural response to our now being in relationship with Him. If we don't have much passion for God coming out of us, perhaps we don't have enough of the Spirit of God inside us.

The early Church did not have books, television, and well crafted evangelism events. Their effectiveness in spreading the good news of Jesus came from a simple and unadulterated passion that welled up from within. The Book of Acts records how thousands of people at a time became Christians, due in no small part to the passion these early believers had for Christ.

Francis of Assisi is often quoted as having said, 'In every situation preach the gospel and, where necessary, use words.' Whilst Francis was largely referring to acts of service, I also believe this statement has application to our passion.

I believe genuine passion is the great persuader. Not merely in our words, but in our whole approach to life ... in our commitment to live exemplary lives that honour God at every turn; in our allowing the joy inside us to emerge on the outside. Not perfect lives but passionate lives, where our love for Jesus and the Kingdom of God motivates and inspires our every word, decision, and action.

lesson number three
Lezione Numero Tre

the italians are hard-working
Gli Italiani Lavorano Duro

3

"Chi dorme non prende pesci" ("He who sleeps catches no fish")

The Italians are incredibly hard working. A 'Skip' asked Luisa's Uncle the other day, 'Why is it that all you Italians seem to own ten houses?' His reply was, 'It's because we all have three jobs ... and by the way your rent is due!'

'Why sit around when you could be working?!' is a highly pragmatic, highly rhetorical question often asked by the Italians.

Over the years of my being an IBM, I have progressively immersed myself in all things Italian. One of my most recent additions has been a foray into the wonderful world of backyard vegetable gardening.

I have a plot in my backyard that was previously occupied by decades-old rootstock roses. After a couple of years of tending them, spraying them, pruning them, fertilizing them - all for the joy of being able to cut a few off twice a year and put them in a vase inside my house, only to have them wilt and die four days later - in true Italian style I found myself asking the question, 'Why grow roses? You can't eat them!' What's more, pruning roses means unproductive work!

So, out they came. Soon after I told this to some avid gardener friends of mine they accused me of breaking the 11th Commandment - 'Thou shalt not throw out old rootstock roses' but I am afraid there is nothing that can be done about them now. (Just for the record I did transplant some of them to my front yard).

Next step was to buy a book on vegetable gardening. My father, who was a full-time gardener for the local council prior to retirement, suggested a reputable guide found in many Australian homes over the years, the 'Yates Gardening Guide'.

Wanting to do it right, and knowing that my every move would be closely scrutinized by Luisa's family, I pored over that guide for weeks, underlining, highlighting, making notes on the margin.

Call me a slow learner but after many laborious hours immersed in the Yates Garden Guide a penny finally dropped for me. Luisa's Grandmother, now eighty years old, has been growing vegetables since she was a very young girl at both her family home in Italy and in Australia since virtually the day she stepped of the boat on arrival in Australia. She has a one-quarter acre block in the suburbs that more resembles a market garden than a residential backyard.

So I threw my Yates Garden Guide away and instead mentally rehearsed my twenty questions for each time we would visit Luisa's Grandmother. "What do you plant this time of year?" ... "What's the best spray for tomatoes?" ... "How far should beans be planted apart?" ... "When should you pick capsicum?" ... "How do you tie up cucumber?" And on the list would go.

Well, after many weeks of my accosting Luisa's Grandmother each time I saw her, she stopped me in my tracks one day, saying, "Marco, this Friday morning you come to my house at ten o'clock, you pick-a me up, you take-a me to your house ... I fix-a everything!" (Yes, my fragile ego did realise this was not so much an offer of assistance but a gesture largely intended as a means of shutting me up!)

Friday rolled around; I did exactly as I was instructed to do (I'm not stupid and I don't have a death wish!). We arrived at my house and there was 'no muck around'. On went her headscarf and her gardening gloves and in the blink of an eye my vegetable garden was transformed into some semblance of hers.

Television has the garden transformation shows 'Backyard Blitz' and 'Backyard Extreme Makeover' ... I had 'Backyard Nonna'! This eighty year-old lady could single-handedly match it with the small army of television gardeners when it comes to hard work!

Because they value hard work and live it themselves, the Italians are always ready to foist that expectation on others.

Melbourne-based Italian-Australian comedian, Frank Lotito, does a great routine on the Italians' perspective of hard work.[9] He talks of his grandmother being confused as to why the contestants on Big Brother (consider yourself fortunate if you don't know what television program I am talking about!) sit around all day with nothing to do. He proposes that a show be created called 'Big Nonna'. On this show there would never be occasions where the contestants had nothing to do ... just the opposite.

The voice would come over the sound system, 'Kids, this is Big Nonna! Come to the back shed-o[10] and help me peel the beans, make the sauce, cook the bread, pit the olives, roll the finnocchio biscuits, pull out the weeds ... '

Luisa's Grandmother reserves the comment, 'She lazy!'[11] as the greatest insult she can throw at someone. You can be a gossip, a bad parent, even a bad neighbour and, while those things are also considered unacceptable by the Italians, they don't rank anywhere near the crime of being lazy.

Australian-Italian comedian, John Baresi, reckons his Grandmother surprised him by telling him how much she likes Formula One driver Michael Schumacher. He was taken aback when she told him this because she doesn't drive a car herself and he didn't know she had an interest in motorcar racing.

He asked her why she likes Michael Schumacher (He assumed it must be something to do with the fact he drives for the Italian Ferrari team) and she said, 'Because he work-a hard ... he has two jobs.' He exclaimed, 'He has two jobs ... which two jobs?!'

'Well,' she said, 'He drive-a the car, the red Ferrari, and he make-a the shoes ... you know, Michael the Shoemaker!' Silly John!

Until recently the Italian language didn't have a word for 'weekend'. Now they do ... the word is 'weekend'. They borrowed it from the English language. OK, I know some of you cynics are under the impression that every day is a weekend for the Italians ... long siestas, lazy mornings gathered in the piazza, however this is very much a myth for the majority of Italians, particularly the older ones.

The truth is they work six or seven days a week, from sun up and to sun down! 'Why sit around when you could be working?!' they will tell you. One of Luisa's Uncles in Cannalonga, Domenico, is 70 years old and continually reminds us, 'I don't wanna work any more!', all the while running a bar and restaurant, building a new house, and doing all sorts of other projects while the sun shines.

A couple of months ago I went to one of my Italian friend's in-Laws house to help them with their tomato sauce-making day. His father-in-law personifies the Italian immigrant ethos of hard work.

For a living he runs a limestone construction business. Now he's not the sort of guy who runs the business from the comfort of an office. Rather he, in his mid-sixties's, is on-site every day, cutting limestone, lifting limestone blocks, and on it goes.

But it doesn't end there. His backyard in suburban Perth is a veritable market garden ... fruit trees, beans, tomato plants, olive trees, and whatever else is in season. No coming home from a hard day's work and putting his feet up ... straight into the garden, digging, pruning, piling manure, picking produce.

My friend, when he was in Italy several years ago, saw a plaque that he could not resist buying for his father-in-law, as it reflects his spirit and work ethic. It is now proudly hung on the wall in the area at the back of the house, where they make sauce. It reads ...

"CHI NON HA NIENTE DA FARE E' PREGATO DI ANDARLO A FARE DA QUALCHE ALTRA PARTE"

Essentially translated ...

"Those who have nothing to do, please go and do it somewhere else."

Why The Italians Are Hard-working
Perche Gli Italiani Lavorano Duro

One thing I love doing is sitting with Luisa's grandmother, listening to her recount stories of life growing up in Italy between around World War 2. During one of these occasions, Luisa's grandmother, who doesn't stand much taller than five foot, described how, as a sixteen-year-old girl, she worked for the local council, picking up rocks to build roads.

The truck driver would collect her and her friends in the morning shortly after sunrise, drive them to their work location, drop them off for the day, and collect them around sun-down ... leaving them to pick up rocks and put them in a pile, all by hand. Luisa's grandmother, together with her girl friends (also slightly built), would carry rocks, balancing them on their heads, some weighing up to seventy pounds (thirty kgs). She tells the story with mixed emotions, proud that she, as a slightly built teenage girl, can boast of having done that yet, at the same time, she makes the point, 'We worked all the time, starve all the time.'

She worked when there was work to do. While she is an incredibly intelligent woman she didn't go to a single day of school in her life ... because the family needed her to work.

Every member of the family was expected to do his or her share to earn an income. They supplemented their income by growing as many fruits and vegetables as possible, selling any excess for whatever price they could get. Additionally, they became very resourceful at making an endless list of their own things, from bread to clothes and so on.

Working hard and constantly during those lean years wasn't a matter of a diligent disposition but of sheer necessity ... fear of starving. The teenage girls stared death in the face each and every day. The cupboards were indeed bare ... living hand-to-mouth was their reality and they knew that if they stopped working they would soon be dead.

This is a hard concept for people like myself, who have grown up in a developed Western country, to grasp. We are repeatedly exposed to the worldview that advocates rest and recreation as life's ultimate goal.

I was at lunch with the family last week, in honour of some friends from Cannalonga who were in Perth for a wedding. During the meal which, as per every special occasion, comprised ridiculous amounts of food, one of the Perth-based friends was telling me of how she had come to Perth with her family when she was only five years old. She strongly made the statement, 'If we hadn't left when we did, we almost certainly would have starved to death ... the whole family.' Motivated by a fear of starving and a faint hope that things would eventually turnaround, the Italians worked hard.

The Apostle Paul wrote, 'If a man will not work, he shall not eat.'[12] Whilst Paul was giving it more as an instruction to believers to pull their weight, the Italian immigrants moved away from Italy because there was not enough paid work for them even to survive in many cases.

Having stared death in the face and then having been given a second chance, these Italians were determined to do everything in their power to craft a new life for themselves.

They seamlessly took this pattern of a hard working lifestyle and carried it on the moment they got off the boat.

Luisa's grandfather did not know a single person and did not speak a word of English when he stepped off the boat. He tells the story of how he was standing on the dock looking a little helpless, when an Australian man came up, to whom it was obvious that Luisa's grandfather was an Italian immigrant who had just stepped off the boat and was looking for a job. Using friendly gestures to communicate, the Australian took him to an area where the Western Australian railroad authority was offering labouring jobs to immigrants.

The rest, as they say, is history. Luisa's grandfather, who came to Australia three years before his wife and daughter, as they only initially had enough money for one ticket, was whisked off to Kalgoorlie and put to work building railway lines.

Now, let me paint a picture of hard work. It is almost always hot in Kalgoorlie, given that it borders on a desert. It is 700 kilometres inland, dust-ridden, and dry. The highest recorded temperature is 46.5 degrees Celsius (116 Fahrenheit). There was little or no machinery except a pick, a large saw and a sledgehammer. As he has told me the stories I have tried to picture in my mind what it must have been like in the height of summer but I know I will never come close to understanding.

However, the reality for Luisa's grandfather was that this is what he needed to do, first raise money to bring his wife and daughter over, and then to raise more money to provide for his family in their new and strange country.

This has been a simple proposition all the way along ... they needed to eat to survive ... in order to eat they needed to work and work hard ... so they worked hard.

Application
Applicazione

The secret to success = Work while others wish.

Many great people have espoused the inherent value of working hard. Voltaire wrote, 'Work saves us from three great evils: boredom, vice and need.'[13]   Theodore Roosevelt said, 'Far and away the best prize that life offers is the chance to work hard at work worth doing.'[14]   Solomon wrote, 'Lazy people want much and get little, but those who work hard will prosper and be satisfied.'[15]   Paul wrote, 'Work hard and cheerfully at whatever you do, as though you were working for the Lord rather than for people.'[16]

The Myth Of Overnight Success

One of the unfortunate pitfalls of modern western society is that our expectations of how fast and easy things should be have rapidly escalated to, in many cases, unrealistic and unhelpful levels. We get angry if the microwave takes more than one minute to heat our meal, forgetting that lesser developed countries may spend the whole day hand-preparing their evening meal ... if they indeed have a meal at all. We get frustrated if we have to wait in line at the supermarket checkout or at the fast-food drive through, ignoring the fact that agricultural countries don't get to drink milk until they have hand-milked their animals, boiled the milk, and let it cool down. We get annoyed when traffic lights turn red and momentarily halt our progress, oblivious to the fact that elsewhere in the world some people walk for hours each way to get to work, the market, or church.

We buy lottery tickets with the hope of becoming instant millionaires, yet can't be bothered starting a weekly savings and investment plan. We take on new credit cards and higher credit limits in order to live a seemingly more affluent lifestyle, wading further into uncontrollable debt. We buy the books that promise we can be slim and eat whatever we want, be fit and do no exercise. Easy is in ... hard is out.

Yet the children's tale of the hare and the tortoise is as true today as the day it was written ... slow and steady often wins the race. That's not to say that you will never win the lottery, never score an unforeseen career or business opportunity, it's just to say that we are not to sit around on our hands doing nothing in the meantime!

It is to say that in the overwhelming majority of cases the overnight successes are very rarely achieved overnight. They are almost always the result of years of hard work and preparation. We see the current frame but don't bother to rewind the tape to see what the plot has consisted of to that point.

I often talk about the 'Point of Confluence'.   The point of confluence explains how rivers actually become rivers. We all know of rivers in our local areas or capital cities, flowing endlessly and powerfully toward the mouth and into the sea, yet we easily forget that powerful force is merely the culmination of the converging of small rivulets in the hilltops, which flow together to make small streams; further down the valley they join to become creeks, then estuaries, then small feeder channels, which eventually join up to become the rivers that we see and know.

This final coming-together point, where the water becomes one single flowing body, is referred to as the 'point of confluence', the point from which the results can be spectacular. Yet the point of confluence and the resulting river would not exist without the progressive contribution of everything that comes before them.

We see the big-screen blockbuster but forget the countless hours that went into making it. We see the highlight reel but forget to watch the making.

Great marriages, great parents, great kids, great friends, great communities, great businesses and great churches are not built overnight. They are the culmination of an ongoing commitment to do whatever it takes, to put in the hard work on a consistent basis for a long time. They are the result of sacrifice, of people forgoing the easy road and, instead, walking the road less travelled.

Was Life Meant To Be Easy?

Modern society has brought with it an illness that exists in epidemic proportions - depression. Whilst I don't want to oversimplify the subject, many cases of depression are the direct result of what philosopher Alain De Boitton calls 'the pursuit of happiness'.

Said differently, people are finding themselves frequently disappointed because life is not meeting their expectations. Their happiness is based on happenings, on situations and circumstances, and when the dice don't roll their way they spiral into depression.

In De Boitton's book 'The Consolations Of Philosophy', he questions whether constant happiness is an obtainable goal and then promptly reminds us that it isn't, by suggesting that all of us will experience one or more (I suggest 'more') of the following things in our lifetime:

- Unpopularity
- Not having enough money
- Frustration
- Inadequacy
- A broken heart
- Difficulties

Of course we are going to experience these things, and in some cases we probably have already, some of them many times over.

The reality is, however, that disappointment is not based on what happens to us but on what we expected to happen to us. In other words, disappointment is the result of an 'expectation gap'.

Since the late 1990's Dr Luca Deiana and his team of researchers from the *Universita' di Sassari* have been conducting research on the part of the world that has the most number of people living over the age of one hundred per head of population - his island of Sardinia, off the west coast of Italy. The purpose of the research was to try and identify the commonalities that cause such a phenomenon.

Not surprisingly, much of it had to do with a diet high in organic fruits and vegetables, low intake of meats and dairy products, moderate and consistent intake of hand-made red wine rich in polyphenols (an antioxidant), and daily physical labour.

Yet the research also discovered on additional commonality which, when I first read it, surprised me ... they share a dark pragmatism towards life. Said differently, they don't really expect life to be good and therefore don't find themselves disappointed or depressed. I acknowledge that it may come across as a little paradoxical, but true nonetheless.

It is claimed that the older people of Sardinia *are* depressed but it is a depression without anxiety. Sardinia has seen a great deal of hardship over the centuries. There have been earthquakes, famines, and a near-endless string of invaders, starting with the Phoenicians and the Romans and continuing through the Spanish, and the House of Savoy.

Along the way the people seem to have adopted the attitude that the various invaders will invariably mess most things up, so they focus their attention of getting on with the job and working with the things they can control, like their own plots of land.

It's similar to the conclusion of a US study in 2004 discounting the role of positive emotions in cancer survival. A relentlessly upbeat attitude has been overrated in our Western society.

Much of modern society is based around the constant quest to walk the path of least resistance. Yet the pot of gold is not always found at the end of that rainbow. Some prizes are discovered at the end of a line of hard work, discipline, determination and persistence. An indomitable will and enduring through difficulties lead us to places that ease and backing down never will.

Robert Frost's 1916 poem, 'The Road Not Taken', is oft quoted and oft true ...

Two roads diverged in a yellow wood,
And sorry I could not travel both
And be one traveler, long I stood
And looked down one as far as I could
To where it bent in the undergrowth;

Then took the other, as just as fair,
And having perhaps the better claim,
Because it was grassy and wanted wear;
Though as for that the passing there
Had worn them really about the same,

And both that morning equally lay
In leaves no step had trodden black.
Oh, I kept the first for another day!
Yet knowing how way leads on to way,
I doubted if I should ever come back.

I shall be telling this with a sigh
Somewhere ages and ages hence:
Two roads diverged in a wood, and I -
I took the one less traveled by,
And that has made all the difference.[17]

This poem, in turn, is what psychotherapist and author, M. Scott Peck, borrowed from in the title of his enormously successful book 'The Road Less Traveled'.

Peck espouses the need for all of us to learn the discipline of delaying of gratification in order to truly achieve a satisfying life ... eating the cake before the frosting.

Now please hear me correctly; I am all for life being great. I firmly believe the promise of Jesus when He promised that all who follow Him could access abundant life here on earth and forever more. We also need to remember He said that we will always have troubles in this world; *constant* happiness is an unrealistic goal.

This is another part of life where we need to understand the 'Genius Of The AND' should be in operation. Disappointment occurs when something or someone doesn't meet our expectations. Our faith in Jesus should cause us to expect great things in this life AND it should not cause us to think that bad things won't happen; that hard work and sacrifice are not necessary. One of Martin Luther King Jr's associates, Andrew Young, makes the point that if you are part of a faith whose leader is often symbolized by His being on a cross, then you have to think that sacrifice is at the core of that faith.

In my experience, and certainly in the experience of the Italians, not giving up during difficult times builds character traits in us that seasons of ease simply would not. Sort of a 'sand in the oyster' situation ... oysters are good on their own but with the addition of a seemingly annoying and intrusive grain of sand over a period of time, something worth much more than just the oyster is produced.

The end result of all of that, I think, is that we hold these seeming paradoxes in tension - recognising that some things in life will come easier than others, that we should enjoy God's favour in increasing measure, greasing the wheels of life if you like, AND that some things worth having will not come so easily, that we will face obstacles and will not be able to take shortcuts.

It's not so much ease and happiness that we should seek after but rather God, His joy, His peace that passes all understanding, and the comfort of His Holy Spirit when we are going through difficult times. A life lived with the favour of God shouldn't always be difficult but it will not always be easy either.

We wouldn't need to follow a God of breakthrough if there was never anything we needed to break through. Yet life throws situations and circumstances our way that require us to battle, to stand strong, to trust God more, to work hard. At all times we must remember that the same God, who made a way for Moses and his people when there wasn't a way, is still ready to make a way for us when there doesn't seem to be a way.

I remember reading the book by Leonard Ravenhill, "Why Revival Tarries", when I was in my first year of Bible College, and one particular statement he made, which I consider to be the summation of the thesis of the book, jumped off the page for me then and sticks with me today. He said, 'I can give you one simple reason we don't have revival ... because we are content to live without it.'

Right now, the countries where the growth of Christianity is breaking out in revival-level numbers are also the countries where the very survival of churches requires everyone to participate, everyone to pray, everyone to work hard. My Mum would always tell me, 'If something is worth having it's worth working for.' Well that's true of strong churches ... what better thing could we give ourselves to than seeing the Kingdom of God built through the local church, to see the bride of Christ becoming ever more radiant?

If we think we are going to see great churches built without hard work and without any inconvenience, forget it. The reality is that if we are going to build strong churches that are going to connect people with the gospel message, it is going to take sacrifice and it is going to take hard work. If you somehow think it is going to be easy all the time, you will get disappointed and it will not happen. The reality of it is that it is going to take hard work.

An essential undergirding principle that we need in our individual lives and in our churches corporately is the old-fashioned quality of determination. Determination gets things done ... sees them through to the end ... pushes through barriers ... climbs over obstacles ... causes us to persist even when it seems the odds are stacked against us.

David was determined when he confronted the lion, the bear, and Goliath. Paul was a big believer in the need for hard work and determination. He wrote to the Church in Thessalonika, 'We hear that some among you are idle. They are not busy; they are busybodies. Such people we command and urge in the Lord Jesus Christ to settle down and earn the bread they eat. And as for you, brothers, never tire of doing what is right.'[18] He twice encouraged Timothy to 'fight the good fight'[19]

Jesus said that, 'From the days of John the Baptist until now, the kingdom of heaven has been forcefully advancing, and forceful men lay hold of it.'[20]

I love the title of Erwin McManus's (Pastor of Mosaic Church in Los Angeles) book, 'The Unstoppable Force - Daring To Become The Church God Had In Mind'. Hard work and determination, woven through things such as faith, prayer, and so on, will cause our churches to be unstoppable forces in our communities and our nations. (By the way, McManus seems to have a bit of a theme going with his books, with others that apply to the need for determination in the individual as well - 'The Barbarian Way:

Unleash the Untamed Faith Within', 'Uprising: A Revolution of the Soul' and 'Seizing Your Divine Moment : Dare to Live a Life of Adventure')

A determined, indomitable will stands when others have fallen, presses on when others have stopped, fights even when circumstances seem insurmountable, achieves greatness where others settle for mediocrity.

As I said earlier, the story of the Hare and the Tortoise is true in many situations ... slow and steady wins the race. The old saying that 'things that are worth having are worth fighting for' could also easily be translated to 'things that are worth having are worth working hard for'.

lesson number four
Lezione Numero Quattro

the family comes first
Prima La Famiglia

4

With the Italians the family comes first or, to say it more accurately, the family comes first - EVERYTHING else comes second!

In fact, the Italians actually have a different definition of family to us 'Skips', which I have progressively discovered in my years of marriage.

Some of you may be familiar with the scale of Italian weddings. Our wedding was relatively small as far as Italian weddings go, we only had two hundred guests ... one hundred and eighty-five on Luisa's side, fifteen on my side! The 'Dings' and the 'Skips'. When I said, 'I do' I thought I was marrying Luisa. Little did I know that I was actually marrying one hundred and eighty-five people!

The family is so important to the Italians that the kids don't move out of home until they get married and even when they do they don't move very far away. The greatest dilemma for a newly married Italian couple is to try and find a house exactly the same distance away from both sets of the parents so as not to offend either *Mother*.

And it doesn't stop there. Right now Luisa and I are living in a weatherboard shack built in 1927, that is so warped and buckled you get seasick walking from one side of the kitchen to the other! We are currently working towards knocking it down (providing it doesn't fall down of its own accord first!) and building a new house on the same block. For this we will need to take out a construction loan with our bank.

My biggest reluctance has been that this construction loan will need to be added to our current mortgage, thus making for some pretty substantial repayments from the outset. I didn't want our biggest decision each week to be choosing between making the repayment or buying groceries.

It was my understanding that you only had to start repaying the additional amounts on the construction loan as the money is used to pay for each stage (i.e. once the concreters need to get paid, you draw that money down from your loan and pay them, and then you begin to pay principal and interest on that amount).

Well, in speaking with my bank manager I was stunned to learn that in a rare gesture of magnanimity the bank only expects you to repay the interest portion of the monies you have drawn down at each stage, and doesn't require you to start paying the principal until the lock-up stage (i.e. when you can move in). When I asked why the banks departed from their usually rapacious approach to lending money he explained that the banks assume you will need to rent another property while your house is being built and they don't want to burden you with principal repayments on top of that.

We haven't started the construction stage and you can be sure I am going to get that in writing from the bank because this deal sounds too good to be true. But what they don't seem to have factored in is a separate approach for an Italian family taking out a construction loan.

You see, while Italian families are in the construction phase there is no additional rent involved. They move in with the parents ... for however long it takes (one of my friends set a record of five years - him, his wife and their two kids ... for free!

And that's exactly what we intend to do. The family wouldn't dream of it any other way. On the one hand the Italians would ask, "Why waste money renting when you can live together rent-free?!" but even more importantly, "What a great opportunity to be together for a year or more!" The family all living under one roof ... a glimpse of heaven to the Italians!

[Note: Please don't show this to the banks in case they add in a special 'Italian Family' clause and reverse their surprising magnanimity!]

In Cannalonga the Pizzolante family has five houses, and - surprise, surprise - they are all adjacent to each other. They don't understand why you would want it any other way. Their doors are always open and everyone is constantly in and out of each house. It took me about a week and a half there before I could work out whose kids belonged to whom. They have a different definition of family.

Italian villages are called *paese* and you refer to the people from your village as *paesani*. Paesani are essentially considered part of your family. About one thousand people live in Cannalonga and many more paesani live in Australia and different parts of the world. Eight years later I am still uncovering people I am 'married to'!

There is very little distinction between the nuclear family and the *paesani*. They are all family.

Why is the Family the Most Important Thing to the Italians?

Perch'e' *La Famiglia* e' *La Cosa Piu' Importante Degli Italiani*

The whole nation of Italy was devastated time and again, going back through the centuries. Italy was never one nation as we know it today but many regions, sometimes fighting each other, sometimes other nations, including the Arabs, Turks, French and Spanish and so on. Over this time all you had was the people in your village and your family. It was a matter of survival.

Then came World War Two, leaving Italy a devastated nation, with survival again being a daily challenge. As pressure and opposition came, as the basic needs in life were not to be taken for granted, everyone in the family had a role, had a part to play in their family's survival.

In Carmine's family, living in a stone hut, one person tended to the goats, another person's job was to draw water from the fountain ... everybody had a role, everybody made a contribution. They learnt what it means to stick together.

In the village each family did what they were good at and then they barter-traded with one another to make sure that no family was in lack. Everyone ultimately had what they needed and, as a result, survived.

When the Italians migrated to places like Australia, they didn't know the language and they didn't know the bureaucratic systems that operated. For instance, they didn't understand the banks so they didn't use them. Italians would keep their money in their houses under their mattresses. A closed economy developed where the money would circulate from one Italian to another and eventually come full circle.

In those times Italians had no use for telephone directories. They talk about *il mio idraulico di fiducia* (my trusted plumber). They also have an electrician *di fiducia*, a bricklayer *di fiducia*, a butcher *di fiducia*, a panel beater *di fiducia*, a tailor or dressmaker *di fiducia*, and on the list of 'trusted experts' in each and every field goes. Strangely, Signor *di Fiducia*'s name is usually Joe or Frank. Over the years this reliance on their *di fiducia* goods and service providers has come to be associated, at least by the Italians, with a certain implied social status ... they don't just buy what the market offers.

Italians have become quite wealthy because they have not spent their money outside this closed economy. But it was never first and foremost about the wealth ... it was a matter of survival. Out of this isolation, both throughout history and since immigrating, they have learnt to put the family first and everything else second.

Application
Applicazione

I think the application is three-fold: The first being how we interact with our families; the second being how we, as Christians, interact with our neighbours and our communities, particularly those who don't know Christ; and the third being how we connect into our own Churches.

Our Families

In English we have two words: 'House' and 'Home'. In Italian there is only one word, *casa*. A house is a building where people live, a home is a place where a family dwells. A *casa* is where the physical and emotional base is. Italians don't understand the separation of the two concepts. They make no such distinction. In fact they have a saying which sums up the primacy of the home and the family, *"In gioia e in lutto, la casa e tutto."* ... "In joy and in grief, the home is chief."

The *casa* is the foundation of everything for the Italians. You might say it is the concrete slab. To misquote Julius Caesar, "We came, we saw, we concreted!"

The Italian approach to many of the everyday aspects of life instinctively involves the family joining together. Take cooking and eating for example. You will often see an Italian Nonna cooking with her daughter, in much the same way as Australian men cook communally on their barbecues. It moves the practice of cooking from a sometimes-lonely chore (if you don't particularly like cooking, that is) to a family activity - something that brings you together, allowing for conversation to flow freely.

When I am in Los Angeles I stay with friends and love to cook for them. Though I don't stand on my own in the kitchen while they frolic in other parts of the house, I try to involve them and their kids in the process. Not so much to share the load but rather to share the experience ... we chop together, we simmer and bake together, we laugh together, and the crescendo of the experience is that we all share in the enjoyment of savouring the spoils of our work. This becomes an hour or two of quality time - we turn off the TV, put on some great music, and love the whole package. Statistics show that families who regularly eat together, because they share more than just the food, are closer.

Contrast this with the results of a study published by USA Today:

"The dining table, once a focal point of family life, is vanishing from British homes due to a lack of space, a preference to eat in front of the television and a rise in divorces.

Sales of dining room furniture have dropped eight percent over the last five years, according to the survey by market research firm Mintel.

In contrast, sales of home office furniture have jumped 40% and those of bedroom furniture by 37% in the same period. Similar research by vegetarian experts Cranks found that almost one quarter of British households do not own a dining table, and of those that do, more than half said its primary function is no longer for eating regular meals.

Traditionally, families in Britain and across the world used the dining table as a meeting point for the family to talk and discuss their day while eating dinner. Many also convened for lunch and breakfast. But the time constraints of modern life, with parents often out of the house working until late, and the temptation of eating dinner in front of the television have eroded this age-old tradition.

Nearly one third of families surveyed by Cranks only use the dining table for special occasions such as Christmas and birthdays. A mere five percent said they sat around it every day, it said.

"Today, dining rooms have become almost defunct as a place where a family enjoys an everyday meal together around the table," said David Bird, a senior market analyst for Mintel on Friday. "For many grazing or eating on the hoof have replaced meal times, while for those who do sit down for dinner, it is often merely a case of a self-service meal eaten on the lap in front of the television or a bite at a local eatery," he said.[21]

FRAME 5/250 EXPOSED

So much of this type of lifestyle change is a reflection of our priorities, a result of a slippery slope that we have allowed ourselves to slide down…and our society is reaping the negative results of this priority shift.

Our Communities

Jesus' final words on this earth were pretty plain, 'Go into all the world and make disciples.' Yet increasingly in modern Western society too many Christians are doing exactly the opposite. Instead of going into all the world we build an overly safe and overly insulated life. We go to the Christian hairdresser, get our petrol from the Christian-owned petrol station, only work for Christian people, and on it goes.

Now, much of this is well intentioned, perhaps deliberately giving our business to people who we know are great financial givers into their local Churches, but to carve out a life where the only people we come into regular and meaningful contact with are Christians means we are missing out on opportunities to build integral relationships with people who don't know Christ. Rather than 'going into the world' we are gradually removing ourselves from the world.

Furthermore, we are allowing a growing Western trend to permeate how we do life. Futurist, Faith Popcorn, coined the phrase 'cocooning', referring to the fact that in Western society we are increasingly withdrawing from our neighbours and building comfortable, impenetrable walls around our houses, from which we only venture to go to work and, upon returning, we draw the blinds and shut the doors. The increasingly popular 'gated communities' are shrinking further to become 'gated homes'.

This is a far cry from the days where the front patio was the gathering place for the family and the ideal place to *ensure* regular interaction with passers-by from your neighbourhood.

These days we proudly quote the proverb, 'Good fences make good neighbours!' We sleep twenty metres away from total strangers. Yet this is not the biblical pattern for believers. How do we expect to impact the world of those around us if we will not open our lives to them?

One of Carmine's side jobs is building fences. When we were in Cannalonga for the first time, Luisa was trying to explain this profession to her uncles, though it was made difficult because the uncles did not understand the Italian word for 'fence'. You see, in Cannalonga, and in so many other *paesi*, their houses are not surrounded by fences. Instead, they are open to any and all who wish to enter, interact and partake of all that is there.

Bill Hybels, in his treatise on contagious Christianity, strongly espouses close proximity as a necessary variable if we are to be used by God to help move unchurched people in their spiritual journey. Makes sense, I know, yet how many of us don't really practise it.

Take this test:

- Do you know the names of the people who live either side of you, including the names of their children?
- Do you know what they do for a job?
- Do you know the ages of their children?
- Do you know what schools their children go to?
- Do you know what their hobbies and passions are?

I'll stop the test there as I am sure you get the point. These sorts of questions are pretty basic yet, if you didn't pass it, then get cracking and, if you did pass it, can you take it further (e.g. Do they have areas in their life where they might need help?). What about answering it for those who live across the road from you? Or those with whom you work? Or the other parents at your child's sporting team?

Our Churches

This cocooning can also creep into our churches, where we simply attend on a weekend but yet have no meaningful relationships with other 'family' members. Said differently, our church experience is based around looking at the face of the preacher and the back of everybody else. Yet this is not the biblical model of church, where we are called a 'body', where our experience should be the face not only of the preacher but of other family members; where we know people and are known.

This played out perhaps the most vividly with a church in Jakarta led by some friends of mine. The Church, Jakarta Praise Community Church, operated in a building adjacent to the Australian Embassy in Jakarta. In September 2004 the Australian Embassy was tragically bombed, an act which in turn destroyed the church premises.

The bombing took place on a Thursday, leaving the leaders to find a suitable venue to hold their services that Sunday ... no easy feat to find a venue large enough considering they had an average weekend attendance of eighteen hundred.

Their Friday was spent frantically looking for a venue, a search that finally paid off, with one of the hotels agreeing to hire their ballroom for an exorbitant fee.

Now the big challenge - letting their people know of the location with less than 48 hours notice. The only method at their disposal was for the staff and key leadership to send text messages to their Cell group leaders and ask them to spread the information.

My friend, Jose Carol, who is the Associate Senior Pastor, told me recently when sharing this story, "It was at that point that we faced this test - were we a Church of people who simply turned up on Sundays or were we a community who were relationally connected? Up to that point we had no way of *really* knowing."

Well, the great testimony is they had three thousand five hundred people turn up to church at the hotel ballroom that Sunday ... not bad for a church of eighteen hundred people! They well and truly passed the test.

Would you and your church pass a similar test? Let's hope it doesn't take a bombing to find out.

I think the closest sentiment we have in English that reflects the primal need for us to have a healthy family environment, where we are loved and accepted unconditionally is, 'Home Sweet Home' and the challenge facing us in more and more ways is to bring this pithy saying and sometimes wall-plaque into reality, where our homes are an oasis in an increasingly challenging world, where our churches are places that feel like heaven welcoming people home.

Jesus said, "Whoever finds his life will lose it, and whoever loses his life for my sake will find it."[22] In other words, it is an axiomatic paradox that, as we commit ourselves to the betterment and success of those around us, our world will indeed benefit. Now our benefiting cannot and should not be our motive yet it is a natural flow-on result. Others come first ... the family comes first ... the people around us, those in Church and those yet to connect with Christ, must come first.

If we live a rapacious, protective life, we will lose our life and the benefits that come from giving it away in the service of others. Yet if we commit to others we will experience life. Marriages where both people are only concerned about themselves are bound for ruin, whereas marriages where each person is committed to meeting the needs of the other will flourish, as both people experience the joy of serving the other and having their needs met in the process.

The Bible describes the early church in Acts Chapter Two, 'And all the believers were together and had everything in common. Selling their possessions and goods they gave to anyone as he had need.'[23] The family of God came first.

A myth I hear perpetuated from time to time is that you can't have intimacy, fellowship and a sense of family in a large and growing church. This belief causes some churches to figuratively close their doors, their philosophy and their not reaching out to people, for fear of losing what they have. It also causes some Christians to avoid being part of growing churches who are reaching out to unchurched people and instead gravitating towards safe and stagnant Churches.

Quite frankly, this line of thinking is a load of rubbish. A sense of family and a sense of intimacy isn't a numbers issue. The Italians can show us this.

After the Second World War Italians were significant breeders. Carmine has five brothers and one sister. Add to that the fact that his family, including nephews, nieces, cousins, uncles, aunts, and so on (not counting *paesani* at this stage), extends into the hundreds. Yet they have built and continue to build a sense of intimacy, a sense of inter-connectedness, a sense of family. Intimacy is not a numbers issue. The great secret is for everyone to be making a contribution.

We need to look at our place in our local church and honestly ask, 'Am I a part of this? Is this my family?' If you want to make it feel more like your family, make a contribution - serve in your church, give in your church, pray for your church.

There would have been no point for Carmine to say, 'I am only 5 years old, I don't want to walk three hours over the mountain with the donkey and get supplies. It's too hard. Get someone else to do it.' It was not about whether he wanted to or whether it was convenient ... he was part of the family and that is the contribution they needed him to make. Day by day the family is built because everyone is making his or her contribution.

Paul wrote, "Speaking the truth in love, we will in all things grow up into Him who is the head, that is Christ. From Him the whole body joined and held together by every supporting ligament grows and builds itself up in love as each part does its work."[24]

Occasionally I have heard people say, "Everything seems to be covered, there's no need for me to serve/give/etc." My response is simply to say that everything may already be covered (though it's too often covered by the usual people doing more than their share to make up the shortfall because they are passionate about their church and the Kingdom) in terms of what needs to be done here and now, but what about the future ... what about the growth of the Kingdom? Jesus said, "From the days of John the Baptist until now, the kingdom of heaven has been forcefully advancing, and forceful men lay hold of it."[25]

You see, the Church is not meant to be operating on cruise control, we are not meant to have a maintenance mentality. Paul reminds us we are in a spiritual battle and we do not war against flesh and blood - that the best form of defense is to attack, to take ground from the enemy, to 'enlarge our tents'.

It is often said that Christianity is only one generation away from extinction ... that if we do not do *everything* we can and place our full trust in God to pass on our faith to those around us, we will lose the battle. As it was for the Italians so it is for us ... a matter of survival!

If we want to see the Kingdom advance and thrive, like the Italians are now doing, we need a greater expression of community, and a greater and richer commitment to one another. We need to look out for the interests of one another ... to do everything in our power to make Kingdom growth an increasing reality.

Growing churches are great places to hide because you can hide among the many new faces. Growing churches, with ministries that are designed to meet people's needs, are therefore great places to have your needs meet without you actually having to make a contribution. Simply attend this, turn up at that.

At Riverview we highly value the fact that people are on a spiritual journey and, as such, we keep our church very 'open at the edges' ... anyone who wants to come can come. They can sit in the back row, check things out from a spectator's vantage point. However we also recognise this should only be an early stage of a person's journey. At some point God requires us to get into the game. If you call your church your home and have decided you want to be a part of that family, God would say 'get off the bench and get in the game and start making your contribution.'

Part of how we build a sense of family in our churches is by putting family first and looking out for whatever needs are required, asking ourselves the question, 'How can I meet those needs? God what have you given me that I can contribute to that?' As you sow into this family it will become and feel more like your family. Jesus said, 'For where your treasure is, there your heart will be also.'[26]

Some of the most connected people in our church have, over years and years on a daily and weekly basis, given themselves into whatever it is they could do to be a part of this family and see our church and God's Kingdom built. Their investment of time, spiritual gifts, prayers, and finances have caused them to have an increasingly vested interest in what happens here at Riverview.

As with large Italian families, being an intimate part of the family is not a numbers game. (I have been part of small Churches where people are disconnected because it was largely a 'spectator sport'.) It is about making a contribution ... it is about being part of this family.

Just as too many people are happy to live in houses inhabited by people but are not prepared to put in the hard work to turn them into homes inhabited by a family, similarly, too many people are happy to go to churches that are simply buildings attended by people but are not prepared to commit their hearts and lives to seeing them become homes of love inhabited by a family.

A house isn't God's best ... a home is God's best. A house was not God's plan ... a home where a family resides was God's plan ... His Church at its best ... His bride at her most radiant.

lesson number five
Lezione Numero Cinque

the italians are resourceful
Gli Italiani Sono Ingegnosi

5

"Il bisogna aguzza l'ingegno" ("Necessity sharpens the brain")

Orson Welles's Harry Lime in *The Third Man* astutely pointed out, "In Italy for thirty years under the Borgias they had warfare, terror, murder and bloodshed but they produced Michelangelo, Leonardo da Vinci and the Renaissance. In Switzerland, they had brotherly love; they had five hundred years of democracy and peace and what did they produce? The cuckoo clock."

"With their gift for snapping back after catastrophe and for making do with whatever is at hand, the inhabitants of Italy have outlived the fall of the Roman Empire; barbarian invasions; raids by Saracens, Normans, and Turks; incessant wars; communal strife; pestilences and floods; famines and earthquakes - and come out all right again and again, their way of life and their closely knit family structure intact."[27]

The longer I have been married and the more Italians I have met along the way, the more I have come to realise that Italians are incredibly resourceful. They extract the most out of everything.

I think this idea of the Italians being resourceful in every area of life is best encapsulated by the Italian expression *furbo*. Whilst in English *furbo* could be literally translated as 'clever' or 'astute', the colloquialism goes far beyond this, and should more accurately be defined as 'slick, foxy, sly, cunning, wily'. Now in English we would equate these words with a slightly derisive picture of someone, however, in Italian, to say someone is or has *furbo* is more often than not of a term of admiration. It describes an ability to get around problems, to navigate a way through difficult situations, to be resourceful in meeting an end goal.

Australian-Italian comedian, John Baresi, tells the story of his grandfather walking into a café. His grandfather asked the barista,

'How much is a coffee?' to which the barista replied, '$2.40.' His grandfather then asked, 'Well how much is the sugar?' to which the barista replied, 'Oh no, the sugar's free.' Upon hearing that his grandfather said, 'Well in that case I'll take four-and-a-half kilos of sugar.'

This, my friends, is *furbo*.

Now don't get me wrong, when taken to extremes, as happens often with Italians, *furbo* has led to lawlessness and quasi-anarchy in many situations, yet in the right measure it is an extremely useful trait to possess. In fact, anyone that has ever dealt with Italian government departments, civil servants or bureaucracy will tell you that *furbo* is the ONLY thing that will get you what you need.

Italy, "The Boot", is a relatively small and infertile land and yet the Italians have become known for producing some of the world's greatest foodstuffs ... pasta, parmesan cheese, tomatoes, Italian sausage, *wine*, olive oil, grapes, tomatoes, zucchini, artichokes, peas, broad beans, borlotti beans, cannelloni beans, cherries, peaches, apricots, nectarines, figs, apples, pears, fine honeys, and on it goes.

You will be hard pressed to see grass growing in Italy. They would say, 'Why grow lawn? You can't eat it.' You see, Westerners grow things to look at ... Italians grow things to eat!

Italians have not only learnt to extract the most out of their land but, more importantly, out of every facet of life.

Most Italian immigrants and older Italians have retained their post-war mentality, where things that work have to be made to go on working, and on and on and on, just as food on the plate has to be finished, not thrown away.

Italians have a saying, '*Non viene sprecato niente*' (Nothing is wasted). Luisa's Grandmother often says much the same thing, 'No throw away!' and 'No waste-a nothing!' There are many examples of how this plays out in the life of the Italians.

Take Italian red wine. Many Italian immigrants make their own red wine and most of it's fantastic. They make it using very simple traditional methods - no fancy equipment and university-trained viticulturalists here. You may have seen the pictures of the old Italians stomping on the grapes in large vats with their bare feet, crushing the grapes and extracting the juice.

What you may not know is that the use of the grapes doesn't end once all of the juice is extracted. At the end of the crushing all the skins remain. Now you and I would probably throw them away because we would now have the wine (and because the grapes smell like your feet) ... task completed. Not the Italians! They couldn't bear the thought of throwing away grape skins so they came up with a clear and highly potent drink called grappa. Quick word of warning ... grappa, she taste-a crappa! The weakest stuff is 49% alcohol content, it singes your nostril hairs as you go to sip it down (if you are overly hirsute that's probably a good thing!).

Then there's lemons. Along the coastal regions of Italy, such as the Amalfi Coast and the Ligurian Coast, you will see spectacular terraces cut into the steep cliffs and hillsides lined with hundreds and hundreds of citrus trees, in particular lemons.

It bears noting that the locals carved those terraces out of the sides of cliffs long before motorized excavating equipment was available.

Now there are many dishes the Italians prepare using these lemons, as well as other uses for the flesh of the lemons but once again, what to do with the left-over skins? 'No throw away!'

Thus came the genesis (and genius) of *limoncello*, a popular lemon-based liqueur served chilled as an after dinner digestive in summer (there seems to be a very direct link between the Italian's resourcefulness and strong alcoholic beverages). The key thing to note is that *limoncello* is not made using the lemon flesh but rather the yellow part of the lemon skin. Very clever and very resourceful those Italians ... the skins of six lemons, when mixed with the other ingredients, makes nearly three litres of *limoncello*.

The bits they don't use for one thing they figure out how to use for something else. When we were in Cannalonga for the first time, because they wanted to show us their great hospitality and generosity they prepared too much food every meal. After three days of having beautiful and plentiful freshly prepared meals for dinner, and then more freshly prepared food the next day for lunch, Luisa asked me, 'Where do you think they are putting the leftovers?' We thought eating leftovers for lunch would save the family the effort and expense of cooking twice a day, and because the evening meal was so nice we were always keen to eat more of it the next day.

But there were never any leftovers served. Yes there WERE always leftovers, but they would mysteriously disappear at the end of each meal, never to be seen again.

We didn't want to be rude and ask the family in Cannalonga, so the first chance we got to solve the mystery was when we rang Carmine back in Australia. 'That's easy,' he told us, 'They feed them to the animals.' No, not the chooks, goats or pigs, but the domestic dogs and cats. No tinned dog food here, Italian dogs eat pasta, chicken, meatballs, goat, and so on.

'Naples, poor in resources, is nevertheless rich in creativity. The pizza was born amid the city's carnival exuberance of life. Nothing, absolutely nothing that can be managed by the human digestive system, is wasted in Naples. During the hungry years of the Second World War, the city's seaside aquarium was ransacked by famished locals who boiled the tropical fish for a variety of unusual pizza and pasta dishes. Neapolitans give this resourcefulness a name - l'arte di arrangiarsi, the art of getting by.'[28]

The 'No waste-a nothing' creed played out when Luisa's grandmother taught me to make bread and pizza. Now it's important to understand a paradox when it comes to traditional Italians and their food.

On the one hand they are very happy to labour over food to serve it to you, and the greatest compliment you can give them is eating a lot of it ... an unambiguous statement that you did indeed enjoy it. On the other hand, as these tend to be recipes passed down through the generations, forged in times of extreme hardship, they are somewhat reluctant to give you a look 'behind the curtain' to the making process and they *definitely* will not entrust their family recipes and the associated secrets to just anyone ... not even an IBM like me! And finally, there is little room for experimentation - learning as you go - because that is equated with the prospect of making mistakes that would run the risk of food being wasted.

No, like the bread itself, I had to go through a proving process before I was allowed to get my hands on. It was a more highly scrutinized process than getting your pilot licence!

One of my first experiences of their life motto 'No throw away!' came in the early weeks of my marriage. Luisa was doing the dishes after a meal one evening (just for the record, before you start thinking of me as some lazy, male chauvinistic pig, we do share household duties ... this just happened to be an occasion when she was doing them and not me) and started to squeeze the last drops out of the dishwashing liquid bottle.

Now I expected, once the last few 'spurts' had been milked, that Luisa was going to simply throw the bottle in the bin. What happened next came as a complete surprise to me.

Instead of throwing the bottle away, she unscrewed the top in a very nonchalant manner, filled it about one-eighth of the way up with water, and put it back in the cupboard for later use. I said, "Babe, where did you learn to do that?" to which she replied in a bemused tone, "Where did I learn to do what?"

You see for Luisa this was an entirely reflex action ... Luisa had grown up watching her Mum, her Nonna, her aunties and, I have since discovered, every other Italian immigrant she knows, adding water to the bottom of a dishwashing liquid bottle so it's good for at least two more washes.

Another example is storage containers. I am an unashamed fan of Tupperware. I think their products are cleverly designed, extremely functional, and the lifetime replacement guarantee adds a high level of assurance to the post-buying process. Tupperware is certainly at the high end of the price scale but I believe you get what you pay for.

Well, you won't see a great deal of Tupperware in an Italian house. Go to their fridge, open a butter container and you are more than likely going to be confronted by preserved olives. When you open the freezer and pull out a tub of ice cream, instead of the contents being what the label suggests you will probably find frozen pasta.

Every Italian family I know has at least two garages ... one for storing hardware, gardening equipment and the like, and the other for storing plastic containers, jars, and bottles. "No throw away!" (Note: The car lives in the driveway ... there is no spare room in the garage!).

And there is a great sense of pride in their resourcefulness. Every year most Italian families have a tomato sauce-making day.

A large number of boxes of tomatoes are ordered, with no-one knowing how many bottles of sauce they will actually end up with.

The operation extends from before sunrise to after sunset and is designed to provide enough sauce for all the family for the entire year.

Bottles are counted throughout the day at regular intervals, as if to convince uninitiated bystanders that they have predetermined targets and quotas, and the culmination of the day is the final count, the grand total.

This final figure is a source (no pun intended) of much discussion for weeks to come:

- 'Gee, we made more than last year!' (Supreme Achievement)

- 'The tomatoes were good this year!' (Read: "We made more than last year.")
- 'The tomatoes were not as good this year!' (Read: "We made less than last year.")

Every Italian will invariably ask other Italian friends, 'How many bottles did you make this year? From how many boxes?' I have observed something interesting about this line of questioning to the broader Italian community:

- The younger generation asks the question to get a feel for the size of the undertaking (i.e. the quotation of large numbers evokes a sympathetic response, knowing that must have been a long hard day's work)

- The older generation asks the question to get a feel for who has extracted the most sauce per box of tomatoes ... a competition to prove who has been the most resourceful that year

Why the Italians are Resourceful

Perche Gli Italiani Sono Ingegnosi

For centuries in Italy, or more accurately, in each region of Italy (Italy has only been a unified nation as such since 1861 - before that it was essentially a patchwork of states), survival was often the main priority. With only a few exceptional periods throughout history, and then only for relatively short periods of time, war within regions, war between regions, and/or war and attacks from other countries were the order of the day. The history of Italy is comprised of centuries of wars, occupations, more wars, overthrows, more wars, re-occupations, and on and on it goes.

Italians were not so concerned about gaining territory, as in the heady days of the Roman Empire, but in defending existing territory from the Spanish, the Turks, the Arabs, the Lombards, the Normans, the Neapolitan Bourbons, and so on. The litany of sieges is woven consistently through the historical time-line of pretty much every region of Italy.

"*Furbo* is a legacy from a long history of political powerlessness, a weapon of the weak. For centuries the people had to humour local princelings and prelates, oligarchs, petty despots, papal legates, Spanish viceroys, French governors, and Austrian generals. To get what one wanted or avoid what one feared, one had to act by indirection, to dissemble, to play a double or triple game. Cunning as a strategy for getting on in life has been cultivated in Italy since time immemorial ... "[29]

The survival of a largely agrarian society is directly proportional to the availability of workable land. Italy is a small country in any case, much of the land is unworkable due to its rockiness, its being too high in the mountains, or its being too close to the sea. Historian Christopher Duggan noted, 'Probably no other region of Europe has produced so many emigrants over the centuries, partly because the population of the peninsula always tended to outstrip the available resources ... '[30]

Yet, when small and varying amounts of land are all you have, then you come up with ways to make it work ... cultivate or die.

When Luisa and I were in Italy in 2004 I went with Luisa's cousin, Joe, who is a veterinarian, to watch him take blood samples of some buffaloes and watch the cowboys round them up (by the way, the Italian word for cowboy is 'cowboy' ... very handy that!), and milk them in order to make 'mozzarella di bufala'. The field where the buffaloes were kept backs onto a seaside cliff, and when

I say 'backs onto' I really mean it. The edge of the field is the edge of the cliff - no boundary fences within a safe distance from the edge of the cliff ... that would be wasting some good metres of land, they would tell me. The cliff was the boundary fence.

The field is on the Campanian coast, about two hours south of Naples, and I was reminded just how prevalent war had been in the history of that and other regions. Also on the edge of the cliff, along with some surefooted buffaloes, was a thirty-metre high fortified stone watchtower. I can honestly say in my ignorance I did not expect to encounter the tower there.

Joe explained to me that the tower is approximately two thousand years old, built by the Greeks when they temporarily ruled the region of Naples, for the purpose of looking out to sea for enemy boats (Turks, Arabs, Sicilians) making their way to Naples.

During the summer the cowboys march the buffaloes up into the mountains to escape the heat, where they live with them for several months. It's not what I would call a pleasant existence for the cowboys but the reality is they have no choice ... go up the mountains or lose the very buffalo that provide your livelihood.

Making the most of what you have, being resourceful, *l'arte di arrangiarsi*, were all born out of necessity and have endured today, woven into the very fabric of what it means to be Italian.

Application
Applicazione

Thoreau wrote, 'A man's riches are based on what he can do without.' Luisa's great grandmother shared the same sentiment when she would tell Luisa's grandmother, 'The poor people can do more than the rich people. We know how to make things from what we have.'

Now when she used the expression 'can do more' she wasn't talking about volume per se but rather about their ability to create things out of very little, using their creativity and resourcefulness. In needing less you are actually getting more. Having less to work with forces you to stretch and multiply what you have, which brings out the best in resourceful people, allows them to exercise their creativity, and leaves them with a greater sense of satisfaction than if everything were readily available.

It's almost as if you 'cheated the system' in a legal way and won ... nobody can steal the credit and nobody can take it away from you.

It's true of the Italians after the war and it's true of people across developing countries today ... when people have a vision of what their future may look like and commit themselves to the mission of seeing that vision realised, you can leave them in a place with nothing and they will prosper. Of course the opposite is also true ... people with no vision and committed to no mission will starve, no matter what resources are available to them. Proverbs says it this way, 'Where there is no vision the people are unrestrained...'[31] For those with a vision and committed to that as their mission, God can do amazing things ... add and multiply in supernatural ways.

We only get one shot at this life on earth and I believe one of our greatest challenges is that of stewardship ... what are we going to do with every minute we have on earth? What are we going to do with the spiritual gifts God has entrusted to us while we are on this earth? What are we going to do with the finances that pass through our hands while we are on this earth?

Are we going to waste things like spiritual gifts, which are given to us for the building up of the Body of Christ? Are we going to waste money on things that are unimportant, because our priorities are out of whack or we lack the discipline to steward our finances wisely? Are we going to throw away the precious commodity that is time, for much the same reasons? I think we need to make the most out of every single moment and every single opportunity.

As a Pastor within a local Church I am confronted every day by the reality that the Kingdom of God, through our local Church, is built the fastest on good stewardship by all those who call Jesus their Lord and call our Church their home.

I am also confronted by the reality that one of the best and most consistent means of ensuring your own personal spiritual growth is through good stewardship. In the Parable of the Talents the increase in capacity came to two people and the decrease to the third for one reason and one reason only ... how they stewarded what was entrusted to them.

In Luke, Chapter 16, Jesus says that for increase to come we must steward three things well - small things, money, and other people's things. He reminds us that if we do our side of the deal well, God will take care of the increase.

Yet too many Christians don't understand the power of stewardship ... what it means for them personally and what it means for the Kingdom.

Champion boxer Joe Louis said, 'You only live once, but if you work it right, once is enough!' For each of us the clock is ticking ... let's ensure we are faithful in our stewardship of everything God has entrusted to us ... 'No waste-a nothing!'

Founder of Opportunity International, David Bussau, is a proponent of the theory he calls 'The Economics Of Enough'. In this he is specifically referring to the challenge to people of means to draw a line in the sand at a point of accumulation of finances and material possessions, beyond which he challenges to use what they have, over and above that line, for the betterment of others. Yet too often, particularly we who live in a comfortable and relatively affluent Western society and have never known first-hand what it's like to have nothing, mindlessly and carelessly waste the excess of what we have.

This can be seen in a variety of ways:

- Overspending on credit cards so we end up spending hundreds of dollars each month on interest payments ... money that we obviously don't get to use in that instance and could have been put to much better use;
- Discarding food that we don't immediately need, either having bought/prepared too much or simply not having been organised;
- Purchasing an endless array of gadgets, 'toys', and items which become 'dust collectors' once the novelty has worn off (usually counted in weeks or, at best, months);
- Making being parked in front of the television our default location in the house and consequently wasting countless hours every week.

In contrast the Italian immigrants walked a very different path:

- The Italian immigrants did not use credit cards ... if they didn't have the cash they didn't buy something. This way they never over-committed and never wasted a cent;
- Many popular Italian dishes, including frittata and various soups, had their origins in left-overs;
- Italian immigrants did not need to have the latest of everything and could often be heard to say, 'This one, she's-a still good!' This very mindset is what made them famous for covering their

couches with plastic, with every intention of keeping them in good condition long after they have become 'unfashionable';

- Italian immigrants watch very little TV. Instead they gather together and talk, thus building community, or get out and work, providing a myriad of obvious benefits.

On the gadgets and 'toys' issue, I couldn't help but find myself bemused and somewhat disappointed when some people we knew, who were recently moving their family from here in Perth back to their country of origin, sent through a list of their household items for sale (i.e. so as not to have to ship it overseas to their destination). It read like a catalogue for a large department store ... there was a least one of everything you could possibly buy and in some cases more than one - 167 various DVDs, popcorn machine, hot dog machine, waffle maker, pizza maker, ice cream maker, seven bicycles - there are only four people in their family - and on and on the list went, for several pages.

I couldn't help but wonder how much of this stuff they actually used and how much of it had to be retrieved from storage and dusted off before putting it on the market. Now of course people are free to spend their money in whatever way they want but that's actually part of the problem.

"Il denaro è un buon servo e un cattivo padrone" ("Money is a good servant, but a bad master")

You see, I think it's a matter of perspective. If we really follow Jesus as the Lord of our life, then our time, our money, our resources are no longer ours but should be submitted to His lordship also. Therefore whilst we have freewill, we are meant to submit our choices to His leading and I think this would result in less impulse spending, less time wasting and instead a greater consideration of the Kingdom in our allocation of our resources.

Money spent on credit card debt could be given to missions or other Kingdom work ... money otherwise spent on 'dust collectors' could achieve the same, without any increase in our income. Or, at a more basic level, I occasionally talk with people who plead their frustration at not being able to tithe 10% of their income, whilst at the same time paying 17% interest on one or more credit cards because they are not living within their means.

Therein lies the challenge. In a reasonably affluent era in Western society we can grow quite lax in our approach to our resources. Our backs are not against the wall ... on the whole we have an abundance of resources and a growing array of options available to us. We are not forced by circumstance to make every moment, every dollar and every possession stretch as far as it possibly can.

Yet what if, despite the absence of the hardship, we adopted the mindset of the Italian immigrants, that there is a sense of urgency and a need to be constantly resourceful. I am convinced the Kingdom would benefit immediately.

Ultimately, I think our strategies when it comes to stewarding our finances need to be both defensive, that is looking for ways to save money, and offensive, that is looking for ways to create wealth. In fact the Bible says it this way, 'But remember the Lord your God, for it is he who gives you the ability to produce wealth, and so confirms his covenant, which he swore to your forefathers, as it is today.'[32]

The point being that it's not so much that God gives us wealth but that He gives us the power to produce wealth, through ideas, inspiration, relationships, and His blessing.

Here are some tips to get you started because after all '*Quattrino risparmiato, due volte guadagnato*' ('A penny saved is a penny earned')

Some Assorted Frugality Tips from the Italian Immigrants

Tip #1 - Just add water

When you get to the bottom of your dishwashing liquid bottle and you think you have squeezed the last few 'blurts' out of it, unscrew the top and add a small amount of water ... it will be good for a few more rounds!

Note: The same applies for shampoo, conditioner, cleaning spray in pump packs, etc.

Tip #2 = "No throw away!"

You won't see much Tupperware in the cupboards and fridges of the Italian immigrants. Look in the margarine container in the fridge ... you'll find olives! Defrost the Chinese takeaway container in the freezer ... it's pasta sauce! Jars of all shapes and sizes are kept and used for storing everything from pasta sauce, dried herbs, homemade jam, sun-dried tomatoes, etc.

This also extends to fabrics. The Italian immigrants keep all old tea towels, bath towels, clothes, to be used for everything ranging from cleaning and dusting rags to tying up trees and garden plants.

If you make espresso coffee in a stovetop machine ('*machinetta*' to the Neapolitans), never throw away any that you don't drink. Instead, put it in a glass bottle with a screw seal (air tight) and put in your fridge. It's great on its own in summer, or poured over vanilla ice cream, or mixed with milk for an iced coffee.

Tip #3 = Turn off all passive electricity draining appliances.

The microwave oven is turned off at the main socket, as is the television, stereo system, and so on. One's sweat pores have to open to a considerable size before the fans are turned on ... let alone the air conditioner!

In fact don't be surprised when you walk into shops in some parts of Italy to find them quite dimly lit, a result of the shopkeeper's desire to keep overheads down by only turning on every third light!

Tip #4 = Buy food in season

In times of poverty, the Italians survived largely by eating what they could grow. The ultimate benefit of this is it caused them to create countless dishes that rely on fresh, seasonal ingredients. Now, in our modern grocery stores, fresh seasonal ingredients are still the cheapest and healthiest options. Said differently, apples will cost you twice as much in summer as they do in winter (and the ones you buy in summer are likely to have been stored in a freezer at the wholesaler for up to a year!)

Can I also encourage you to make your own jam (using the fruit in season) and preserve vegetables such as capsicum and zucchini. The jam is dead easy and tastes better than the chemically enhanced stuff you buy in shops (which contains very little fruit!) and the preserved vegetables are great with bread for either antipasto or as a simple lunch. In the Book of Proverbs it says 'Ants are creatures of little strength, yet they store up their food in the summer'. Wise advice that!

Tip #5 = Never pay retail

Whether it be food, clothes, appliances, motor vehicles, or whatever ... the Italians will insist that you *never pay retail!* They will hold out for months before making a purchase, waiting patiently until the price is reduced. They will drive an extra ten kilometres to save five cents a packet for pasta. They will haggle at the checkout of their local supermarket, insisting they deserve a discount because they are a regular customer and they are paying cash!

It might seem strange to those of us who are accustomed to impulse buying and forking over whatever the price tag says we should pay but if you think about it, over a lifetime, you would invariably save tens of thousands of dollars as a direct result of the stubborn and endless quest never to pay retail.

Tip #6 = You don't always need the best

In most Italian houses you will find two types of toilet paper - the cheap and nasty one that is single-ply and more resembles sandpaper than toilet paper, and the nice, soft, three-ply variety which they will quickly swap onto the roll when they have visitors.

The same goes for coffee, glassware, and biscuits - cheap variety for the family and the nice stuff for the visitors.

But it's the principle that I like - you don't always need the best. You might think that this is being cheap, not frugal, however my friend Phil Baker says it best:

- Frugal is buying generic brand sugar
- Cheap is buying generic brand coffee

Tip #7 = Buy only what you can afford

Too many people are drowning in credit debt - be it their store cards, credit cards, personal loans, or a combination of all of the aforementioned. Banks and department stores are becoming increasingly generous, making credit easier to come by, allowing people higher credit limits and, in more and more cases, issuing new credit cards without any formal verification of a person's earnings or their credit history.

Whilst I personally find this practice abhorrent and believe that financial institutions should be more about serving their customers by working with them to ensure they don't get into trouble rather than making credit available beyond a person's ability to pay it back, I also realise it is the responsibility of each individual to consider their own position.

Whilst the Italians were forced to buy only what they could afford, as it was the days before credit cards, most of them have maintained the discipline and, as such, live debt free and, in turn, worry free.

Tip #8 = Squash your toilet rolls

Many an Australian has gone into an Italian family's toilet and have been surprised to discover that the once-round toilet roll is now more oval in shape, the cross-section of which is shaped like an American football. Well, it makes sense when you think about it. When you tug on the toilet roll it is very easy for it to spin in perpetuity, leaving you with far more paper in your hand than you really require. By squashing the roll before putting it on the holder it reduces the rate of spin and ultimately produces a sort of braking effect after only a few revolutions, thereby automatically hedging against wastage.

Over a lifetime the savings really add up!

Tip #9 = Buy in bulk and save

Don't just buy one tin of canned tomatoes when you go to the supermarket (i.e. for those without their vegetable garden); when they are on special buy a couple of boxes. When you see pasta or washing powder at half-price, stock up. These sorts of items don't have 'Use By' dates and while it may seem you are increasing your shopping bill that week and denting your cash flow, over many months of cultivating this habit you will find you are spending less overall.

lesson number six
Lezione Numero Sei

the italians are expressive
Gli Italiani Sono Espressivi

6

"We find the short-haired wool of our speech very unlike the silky and ductile fleece of that of Italy." Thomas Campbell, Life and Times of Petrarch, 1843

Italians say, 'Why use a hundred words when a thousand will do?!' They know how to express themselves well ... and then some!

In Indonesia recently a tribe was discovered high up in the mountains that had remarkably had no previous contact with the outside world. Another surprising thing was that their language consisted of only one syllable. I think if you were to tell my Italian in-laws that they could only communicate with one syllable they would most likely say, "Shoot me now!"

Language and expression play such a central part to the lifestyle of the Italians that even Italian school and university exams are largely verbal exams rather than written, where students are required to stand before a panel and answer questions. I think that would frighten the pants off many non-Italians, where the sheer terror of the experience alone would lead to their ultimate failing, their memory banks erased by fear of public speaking rather than a lack of preparation and study.

Italians love to talk and love to express themselves. Not only is it impossible to speak Italian without moving your mouth, it's probably accurate to say it's impossible to speak Italian without moving every other body part as well!

An Italian has his mouth flapping around, his hands flapping around, his head rolling, shaking and nodding, fingers doing strange gestures, and hands loudly slapping on thighs. My advice to you is not to invade an Italian's personal space when you are having a conversation because you will probably get hurt.

Another example is laughter. Laughter is rarely restricted to a polite giggle. In fact it seems Italians have an inbuilt mechanism that automatically triggers involuntary hysteria.

I love telling Italians a joke because the way they respond to the punch line, with their whole body convulsing, makes you think you are the next Jerry Seinfeld. I told Carmine the following joke the other day and I thought he was going to pass out (gauge your reaction against his):

Q: "Why does Pavarotti sing by himself these days?"
A: "Because he ate the other two!"

Now, I think the joke is 'smile' funny but I hardly needed a defibrillator the first time I heard it!

Then there's talking on the telephone. I have discovered that the volume Italians speak at on the telephone is directly proportionate to their distance from the person they are calling. For an inter-suburban telephone call within the metro area an Italian speaks at only slightly higher volume than that of a 'Skip'. However the exact same conversation back to Italy can actually be heard by the family in Italy *without* the assistance of a telephone.

When Luisa's grandmother makes a call to her family in Italy I have to remind her that she has a phone near her mouth and they have a phone next to her ear. (All this is even more ironic to me given an Italian invented the telephone in the first place!)

And of all the Italians, I came to be married to a Neapolitan. The people from the region of Campania are famous for being the loudest and most expressive of all Italians. In the words of Spinal Tap, their volume control 'goes up to 11!'

Neapolitans are extroverts. All their gestures and statements are outgoing. Nothing is held inside. In fact the Neapolitans have an expression, *"Se non si canta sei morto"* ... "If you don't sing you're dead". I've yet to figure out if that means a lack of singing will kill you or a lack of singing is a symbol that you are already dead (on the inside that is) - perhaps it's both. In any case, it encapsulates the Neapolitan's outlook on life, that it should be lived expressively.

In fact the Neapolitans are so famous for their expressiveness that, in Naples in 1832, the Canon of the Cathedral of Naples, Andrea Di Jorio, wrote what has come to be regarded as the first ever book on semiotics, the study of body language, called *'La Mimica Degli Antichi Investigata Nel Gestire Napolitano'* ('Gesture In Naples And Gesture In Classical Antiquity'). This book focuses on everything from the very subtle tilting of the head, which has a particular range of meanings depending on the direction, length and/or ferocity of the movement, to the hand and arm gestures that are guaranteed to leave foreign passers-by spellbound on a stroll through Naples.

My first exposure to a Neapolitan gathering was like being run over by a Mack truck! I remember witnessing my first conversation around the table where everyone gathered was speaking in Italian the whole way through. There were some uncles, aunts and other friends who hail from their village with us at the dining table ... they were all talking loudly (i.e. they were all shouting), they were all speaking at the same time, and they were all waving their hands like crazy.

At the time I did not understand a word they were saying but I was still fascinated by it all and sat mesmerized, trying in vain to take it all in. However, after ten minutes my fascination turned to fear and I felt I had to leave the table for self-protection. The volume, pace and the level of their physical demonstrativeness continued to escalate like the Cuban Missile Crisis. I thought the whole episode was going to end up in a fight!

Later on I discovered that, while there *were* parts of the conversation where people were a bit heated, for most of it they were just expressing themselves on a variety of topics. It was incredible. Coming from a polite Australian home where you took turns speaking, would never dream of interrupting, and would actually wait until there was a noticeable pause by the person who was speaking at the time before you opened your mouth, just to ensure they had indeed finished what they were saying and weren't merely taking a breath.

I had never experienced anything like it. They all spoke at the same time yet somehow they all listened at the same time (I'm not sure if you know this but over the centuries Italians have genetically adapted to be able to breathe through their ears so they can talk without pausing!) ... and what struck me the most is that somehow they all remained friends at the end of it! But the fact is this was just an everyday conversation for them ... it was so commonplace that nobody but me would even remember it.

It's also great to be a baby growing up in an Italian family. Now I know all families love having little babies around and are eager to express their affection. But I can assure you this expression of affection is scaleable between cultures and that Italians know how to express it on a grand scale.

For a nice, reserved and orderly family like mine you would be more likely to pass the baby around to the family members for a few minutes each, where they would get to make a few gestures towards the baby ... not too over the top because you don't want to look like an idiot.

It's a different set of rules when it comes to the Italians I can assure you! Italians are completely unconcerned about what anybody around them thinks when it comes to expressing their affection towards babies (and expressing anything come to think of it!).

I was with some friends of mine, the Rossis, at their family's annual sauce-making day recently, where one of the sisters had her twin baby boys. I have never seen anything like it. No stopping at a simple "Gitchy, gitchy, goo!" for these Italians. Those babies were given the full treatment ... cheek pinching, kisses with mouths so demonstratively poised that at times I thought they were going to eat the babies, cuddles that would have rendered a bagpipe unusable, and on it went. The biggest challenge that day when the twin babies were around was to keep everyone focused on the task at hand ... making sauce!

As Tim Parks pointed out, 'It's what the Italians enthusiastically call *fare festa a qualcuno*, which, literally translated, means "to make a party for someone", and combines the ideas of welcoming them and smothering them with physical affection. Comparison of this expression with the slightly disapproving "to make a fuss of" speaks worlds about the difference between Italian and English approaches to such occasions.'[33]

Then, of course, Italians are famous the world over for crying. I recently went to a wedding between two of my Italian friends and from my vantage point in the wings of the church I watched as the bride walked down the aisle. Almost like a series of dominoes one row of Italians after the next unashamedly and unreservedly starting crying.

Now I know other cultures cry at weddings, but few on this scale and few with the outward appearance of seemingly rehearsed military precision of the Italians. The Mexicans are credited with having 'invented' the 'Mexican Wave' ... perhaps the sequential opening of tear ducts at Italian weddings should be called the 'Italian Wave'.

It's important for us to understand that the Italian's disposition towards shedding tears is not a genetic one, as if they have more and/or bigger tear ducts than anyone else, so much as a cultural one. In the West we often associate crying with weakness, especially for males. The Italians associate *not* crying with weakness, as if you have no heart and no feelings.

If they feel it, they don't hold back.

Why The Italians Are Expressive
Perche Gli Italiani Sono Espressivi

Quite frankly I have found this trait, along with passion, to be the most difficult to give a valid explanation for. As with passion, many have said it is in the blood, which I am sure is true, though I have not been able to fully accept that this is the only explanation.

American scholar, Adam Kendon, who in 2002 translated Andrea de Jorio's seminal 1832 work into English, offers his own theories on why the Italians, in particular the Neapolitans, are expressive. His key reasons are:

'We suggest that, from a complex combination of factors, including the physical conditions in which most people lived, the prevalence of "home industry" in the city, the high level of crowding, and the character of the climate that allowed people to remain outside very comfortably for much of the year, over many centuries a particular style of urban life developed in which, for much of the time, people were always co-present in spaces only partly well-bounded or screened, not only with members of their own family but also with others, most of whom would at least have been acquaintances. Life, all facets of it, tended to be carried out within a complex set of overlapping settings, always in the presence of a widening range of possible witnesses ... I suggest that these conditions ... led to the development of a range of communicative strategies which favoured the use of gesture, at once for its properties as a mode of display, for its usefulness as a silent mode of communication in circumstances too noisy for speech at a distance, and, on the other hand, its usefulness as a medium for concealed or 'side' communication. It also makes it possible to maintain more than one axis of communication at a time.' [34]

Kendon then goes on to underscore de Jorio's observations of quarrels:

'No one is spared the roughest curses and shouts of the two quarreling parties and they are always uttered in such loud voices that not a single syllable is lost on anyone around. Gestures make up for what cannot be heard by those too far away. When the quarrelers separate, they are still shouting and they continue their curses and imprecations even when mush distance separates them ...' [35]

Kendon then takes this and underscores a further observation made by de Jorio:

'Naples in de Jorio's day was notorious for the density of its population. In such circumstances, where several different

behaviour settings occupy the same physical domain at the same time, individuals must compete with one another for attention. Further, because they are likely to participate in more than one behaviour setting at a time, they must be able to monitor multiple sources of information simultaneously. These conditions, it is suggested, could encourage an elaboration of gesture in the various communicative functions ...'[36]

Both de Jorio and Kendon offer more theories, however I will leave it to you to track down a copy of the book should you wish to read more.

I would like to turn my attention to a theory I have developed which is not limited to the Neapolitans and I think has greater relevance to how we should live our lives in this day and age.

Psychologists, psychotherapists, and those in the counseling profession talk about masks, the facades we create over time and hide behind in most circumstances and in front of most people. The images we like to present to the world around us to give the impression that we are better than we really are, that we have it together more than we really do.

Some of these masks are carefully crafted over time while others are more the result of us developing subconscious behaviour patterns. Whatever the process, masks prevent us being fully ourselves and from expressing our innermost feelings in an unfiltered way.

Recognising these masks can be difficult enough but dealing with their removal is a whole 'nother league. Months of appointments and thousands of dollars have been the path many have trodden in an effort to remove the mask ... with mixed results.

Advice and theories abound on how to best deal with masks but there is one that garners almost 100% agreement ... great personal crisis is one of the most, if not the most, effective ways of forcing our masks to crumble.

When someone has 'been to the bottom', saving face is no longer a high priority. Being yourself, celebrating the little you have, embracing those around you whom you love, treasuring every moment in a pure and unadulterated way - these fast becomes priorities.

Whilst I don't want to oversimplify things, I believe one of the reasons the Italians are expressive is they feel they have nothing to hide, nothing to protect. They have experienced having nothing at times. At other times they lived with the constant threat of losing the little they did possess. In these circumstances they learnt to appreciate what really mattered.

When you have overcome the fear of losing what you have, protection is no longer a priority. With this comes a freedom to bare your soul, express your emotions, throw caution to the wind with little or no regard of what people might think or say.

Application
Applicazione

Expressiveness definitely has its place in the lives of Christians. Jesus wept, he got angry in the temple and let loose with a whip, and he screamed out to God when the situation got too much. Of course, this kind of expression is tempered by self-control and Jesus used the appropriate expression at the appropriate time.

On the one hand we are not meant to be emotional roller coasters, with wild swings that cause us to become unreliable. On the other hand we are not meant to 'flat-line' our way through life, with suppressed emotions submerged like an iceberg below the surface.

At my home church, Riverview, we occasionally receive letters from visitors from other churches complaining that " ... your church has rock music and people are moving their bodies during praise and worship!" and "This is the House of God so there should be more respect." (Read: 'Less noise').

I think where these people are off-track is they have embraced the 'tyranny of the OR' ... that because one of the ways we are to express our worship to God is facilitated through upbeat music and joyous celebration, we are somehow being disrespectful. They seem to be unaware of the litany of references in the Psalms where believers are encouraged to offer praise with clanging cymbals and banging gongs. When you read through the bible you see plenty of people danced before God ... they actually couldn't contain themselves.

I believe those people are only looking at one side of the coin, or not embracing the 'genius of the AND'. That is, the range of ways we are to express our worship to God should span a broad spectrum. There are definitely times for quiet and solitude, for getting on our knees and bowing before the King and there are definitely times for celebration and jubilation. It's impossible to do both simultaneously and our expression should encompass both in their different ways at different times.

I agree that a church that *only* expresses itself in a loud and gregarious way has swung the pendulum too far, just as I believe that churches who *only* express themselves to God in quiet adoration have swung their pendulum too far the other way. I have walked into some churches where I think people are being quiet because they are afraid they might wake God up!

It's encouraging to reflect on that fact that Charles Wesley received this same kind of criticism when he introduced pub tunes into his church services, where he merely changed the lyrics of popular pub songs to make them hymns sung during worship. Whilst it was considered scandalous by his critics it seems God wasn't totally put off and delighted in the praises of at least some of the 'pub tunes'. Ever hear of a song called 'Amazing Grace'? Wesleyan pub tune!

The point isn't so much the tempo but the spirit of our worship.

Or I come across articles by ill-informed journalists (and in some cases leaders of other Churches) leveling the criticism that contemporary churches like Riverview are just based on emotion.

Well I unequivocally disagree that I churches like Riverview are based solely on emotion but I think God would want us to include our emotions in our worship of Him. Jesus said that we are to give God all of our worship, our mind, our spirit and our emotions.

In this aspect of our worship we also need to embrace the 'genius of the AND'. Christianity is not solely a mental exercise, where we call ourselves Christians purely because of a set of beliefs we hold to. Nor should our faith only be lived out in 'the spiritual realm', where we fail to put our faith into action while on this earth. And nor should it be just an emotional experience, where we look to God merely as a source of making us feel good.

There are ditches on both sides of the road. Christians whose only form of expression of worship to God is swinging from the rooftops are missing out on some of the wonder of stillness and quietude in which we can hear the still small voice of God and express our thoughtful adoration to Him.

Conversely, Christians whose only form of expression to God is morose and lugubrious need to 'espresso' themselves in order to better express themselves. There are times for quiet reflection and there are times for raucous celebration.

The area of communication is also so important. Its importance relates to many areas of our lives, including:

- **Conflict Resolution** - where Jesus tells us that if someone offends us *we* are to go to *them*, we are to communicate. Yet too many people bottle things up inside, allowing the offence to gradually eat away at them on the inside, over time destroying their peace, stealing their joy, and ultimately robbing the Church of unity between two people

- **Sharing Your Feelings** - Many cultures have not cultivated, and indeed some have quashed, the art of communicating feelings. Clinical psychologists will tell you that an inability to communicate what is going on inside you to people you love is one of the greatest causes of mental illnesses such as depression, which is growing to epidemic levels on some parts of the world, especially Western countries.

So don't be a Westerner and stew ... be an Italian and spew! Dedicate to communicate. With Italians you'll never understand whether they're arguing or not. They have developed the ability to argue without being angry. It's a healthy trait that we can cultivate in our lives.

Matthew Fort refers to the Italian's ability to talk non-stop as 'logorrhea'[37]. In Australia we have an expression, 'verbal diarrhea', though it is intended as a put down to someone who talks a lot but says nothing worth listening to. 'Logorrhea' is not so much an insult as a compliment. Like the aqueducts in Rome, which have spouted continuous flows of water for two thousand years, so is the Italian's ability to speak without respite.

The priority of communication was driven home to me when we were in Cannalonga for the first time. Every evening, once the meal had been eaten, the table was cleared and then pushed against the wall. Everyone would bring their chairs into a sort of circle, and they would continue talking for hours. No retreating to the lounge room, no splitting off and doing your own thing, no watching television. The instinct and the priority were for more communication.

I think the primacy television has gained in western culture is one of the great social evils of our day. I'm not advocating aestheticism but rather encouraging us to rediscover the dying art of communication, both in quantity and quality. We need this in our families and we need this in our churches.

You can't build deep and meaningful relationships with people about whom you know very little, particularly the stuff inside them. Deep wells of relationship, love and trust are dug over time and require intention and effort. An essential tool for digging the wells of relationship is the willingness to communicate and to open up your innermost being.

I think this is one of the key reasons God has dialed up the small group revolution throughout the church world in recent years. Too many Churches had become places where you went for an hour or so on a Sunday, looked at the face of the preacher but the back of everybody else.

But this is not the picture or the model God has of the church. The Book of Acts tells the story of the early church, a group of believers who met together regularly, who ate together regularly, who shared their possessions in common with one another. In the context of all of this was communication, expression, and the development of deep and impacting relationships.

The community itself was one of the key tools God used for evangelism in those days ... people wanted 'in' on that community. As the Church, if we lose this it is at our peril, the peril of souls that need saving and therefore the peril of the Kingdom.

epilogue

One of my favourite, and I think one of the most challenging, chapters in the Bible is Malachi Chapter Three.

Now many times when we read from Malachi Chapter Three we focus on the section on tithing and on testing God, however the context of the Chapter is all about God calling His people to return to Him, to return to living His way, according to the decrees and principles He has laid before them.

The culmination of the challenges God lays before them is His assurance that, if they do what He says in the way He says, the result will be a life that is better than they could imagine.

In Verse Twelve God goes on to say, 'Then all the nations will call you blessed, for yours will be a delightful land.' And then the crescendo in Verse Eighteen, 'And you will again see the distinction between the righteous and the wicked, between those who serve God and those who do not.'[38]

When I read Malachi Chapter Three I cannot but help thinking of the Italians. They have put into practice the principles I have talked about in this book and, as a result, we call them blessed and we certainly say that theirs is a delightful land ... and there certainly is a distinction between them and people from many other countries.

In fact, this distinction has even been given a name ... 'la dolce vita', the sweet life, living life the Italian way. The Italian way of life has stirred up envy in innumerable people.

I believe it is this sort of envy that God is suggesting should be normal for believers who live according to His word and His ways. That our lives should result in unchurched people wanting what we have, envying our lives and, in turn, begging us to let them know our 'secret'.

The early Church we read about in the Book of Acts reflects this. A large part of their evangelistic effectiveness was the result of people wanting in on whatever it was that was making the difference in their lives. We read in Acts Chapter Two that as the early Church lived according to God's Word and his principles that found themselves, ' ... enjoying the favor of all the people. And the Lord added to their number daily those who were being saved.'

The early Church did not grow solely by people preaching or by evangelistic 'crusades'. Its growth was always undergirded by the fact that unchurched people saw the distinction between the righteous and the wicked, between those who served God and those who did not.

I think often the reason our evangelistic efforts can seem so difficult is that our lives really aren't that different from non-believers. Too many testimonies go something like, 'My life used to be the envy of all my friends but then I became a Christian ...'

Jesus has promised, ' ... I came so they can have real and eternal life, more and better life than they ever dreamed of.'[39] Eternal life with Jesus starts here on earth when we commit to follow Him. His promise of 'more and better life' is both for heaven and for earth.

The difference He makes in our life should be outwardly evident, a distinction, and it should be compelling to non-Christians. Along with prayer our own lives should be the greatest tool we have at our disposal for evangelism.

Jesus plan for us is that we should have the Spirit of God alive and growing in us in such a way that it is flowing over to touch and impact other people's lives. One of the things that has always struck me about Jesus is that everybody - from children, to women in adulterous relationships, to rich people and poor people alike - was drawn to Him.

The interesting thing is I have never had any trouble inviting people over to Carmine and Josie's house for a meal, in fact there is a waiting list (I am considering selling memberships for a bit of extra pocket money!). If we embrace these characteristics of Italians and more besides then we shouldn't have any trouble inviting people to be part of this family. Acts 2: 47 it records the fact that the early Church grew in favour with people and the Lord added to their number *daily!* Christians, despite being persecuted by the people in those times were actually attractive people to be around. People came to be part of those churches, to be part of that family.

Poet Robert Browning wrote, 'For sudden the worst turns the best to the brave.'[40] This has indeed been true of the Italians. For so many years they lived on or below the poverty line, yet their resourcefulness, hard work, sense of family, generosity, and zest for life kept them alive and, over time, has taken them above the line and climbing still.

In some areas of the world, in some cities or in some neighbourhoods, the Church is on or below the line inasmuch as it is not thriving the way that God intended. I believe that as we apply the qualities of the Italian family, which of course are very biblical, we will see our churches turn around.

And then the challenge will continue, though it may very well be a challenge not to grow complacent. When we think we have 'enough' we can be lulled into thinking we will always have 'enough', forgetting what it was like to have had little or nothing, and ignoring Paul's exhortation. 'Let us not become weary in doing good, for at the proper time we will reap a harvest if we do not give up.'[41]

It's interesting to observe that in the absence of severe hardship and persecution, the Italians have continued to live by the very qualities that got them through centuries of extreme hardship and the trajectory has continued to trend upward. Whilst they fought hard to keep their lives 'above the line' for so many years, they have now been catapulted into growing affluence.

The children of immigrants now enjoy a quality of life that is often better than their non-Italian friends, due to their parents' application of the lessons I have shared in this book.

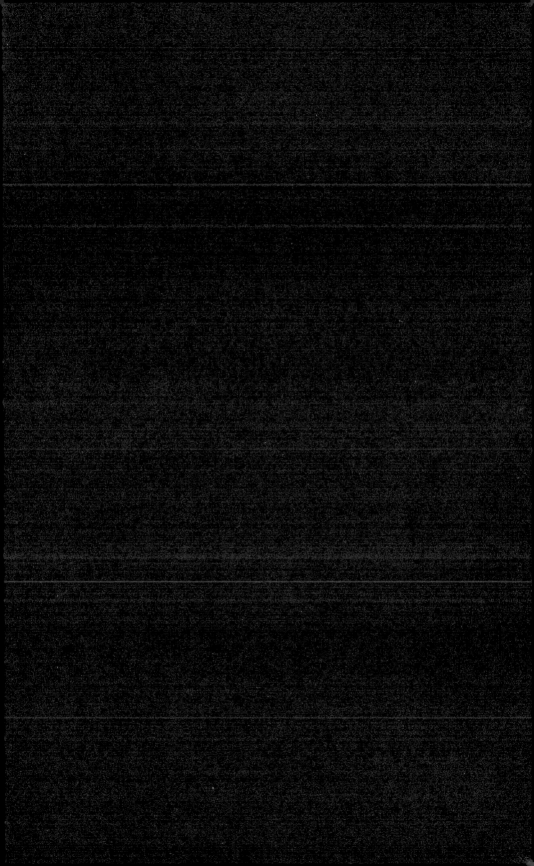

food & recipes
Cibo e Ricette

Italy is, and Italians are, synonymous with food. *La dolce vita* (the sweet life) is often indistinguishable from *la dolce eater!* Westerners eat to live ... Italians live to eat!

It was with this in mind that I felt a book about living life the Italian way just wouldn't be complete without at least a little attention given to food. Thus I have included some Italian cooking tips as well as a few of my favourite recipes.

And it's not so much the quantity of food that Italians love ... it's more about the quality of the food. Whilst many Italians will put up with bad government they will not tolerate bad food. Most Italians would tell you that a small serving of a top quality ingredient is more satisfying than a large serving of a second-rate one.

Italians give attention to the quest for the freshest seasonal ingredients. Combining them to make delicious meals that surprise and delight the taste buds has over many centuries developed into an art form. If you were to ask an older Italian what she would do if she wanted strawberries in winter she would likely give you a puzzled look, simply because she wouldn't 'want' strawberries in winter because strawberries aren't grown in winter. As I mentioned, their passion is for fresh, seasonal ingredients. Italians would say, " ... *se no, ti fa male lo stomaco!*" (If you don't eat things in season, you'll get a stomachache!)

And it's not just the food in and of itself - meals are also an occasion to experience community ... food is meant to be enjoyed together.

In fact the tradition and priority among Italians, for the primacy of enjoying food and enjoying community whilst eating food, was highlighted in recent times by the birth of the Slow Food Movement.

In the early 1990s a travesty of national (and Italians would argue 'biblical') proportion occurred in Italy. In the *Piazza Di Spagna*, at the foot of the Spanish Steps, one of Rome's most famous, most beautiful and most historic locations, McDonald's opened for business - a company whose philosophy of food and eating went against almost everything the Italians hold dear.

In response, several prominent academics, lead by Carlo Petrini, started a revolution. Thankfully not in the form of a group of crazed Italians wielding arms against unsuspecting McDonald's burger cooks but a growing movement of Italians wielding a saucepan and a knife and fork, determined to preserve the values of high quality, fresh ingredients, and the communal aspects of eating, or as they say, to "put the slow back into eating".

My preference when it comes to Italian food is for *la cucina povera* ... the food of the poor, otherwise referred to as *la cucina rustica*, old-style food, where simple is preferred.

Thankfully, true *cucina povera* has resisted internationalization over the years. These are the foods so many of us have since come to know and love in traditional Italian restaurants ... from focaccia and frittata to simple pizza and pasta, using fresh, seasonal ingredients in basic yet creative ways to concoct dishes bursting with colour and flavour. It doesn't always seem 'special' to look at but all the flavours, in the right mix and quantity, are incredibly hard to achieve and are the result of centuries of creativity and experimentation. When zucchini were the main item at their disposal for two months and tomatoes the main item at their disposal for up to five months, they learnt to use their imagination in their preparation.

Remember, Italian is a mindset. So to cook Italian, think Italian, which means treating the fewest possible ingredients with the greatest possible respect.

I have categorised the recipes into the four seasons of the year. These are not hard and fast rules but take into account the fact that due to modern transportation, refrigeration and storage methods we are becoming increasingly disconnected with what is and isn't fresh (although the prices are generally a giveaway ... cheapest when freshest!).

So take time to enjoy the food. Take time to enjoy the people around you. Never eat alone. Never eat on the run. Use these culinary moments to build relationships with your family, your friends, and your community. Don't just feed them ... involve them in the process. Savour the time ... savour the flavour!

Oh yeah, one more thing. Don't get too hung up on the 'low-carb' deal. If you want to ensure you don't put on weight, it's calorie deficit you need each day (i.e. burn more than you consume) ... carbs aren't the enemy, excess calories are. In the first years of dating Luisa I put on about 17 kilograms of healthy Italian 'love'. But it wasn't because one plate of pasta is fattening, it's because four plates of pasta are fattening. (You will be glad to know that I have since regained touch with reality and know how to control myself!)

Do some regular exercise, don't always overeat, and then you can buy into the old Italian saying, *'Una tavola senza pane e' come un giorno senza sole.'* ('A table without bread is like a day without sunshine.')

The Italian Pantry

"A tavola non si invecchia"

"At the table with good friends and family one does not become old"

Whilst Italians lean heavily towards fresh seasonal ingredients, they are backed up by a supporting cast of staples that one must have on hand at all times in order for the culinary symphony to be a success.

So get out your checklist and let the journey begin ...

Olive Oil *(extra virgin and a lighter one as well)*
Vinegar *(balsamic and white)*
Salt
Pepper *(whole peppercorns in a mill, not the powder version that makes you sneeze!)*
Butter
White Wine
Onions
Garlic
Dried chilies
Potatoes
Tinned tomatoes *(for when they are out of season)*
Olives *(green and black)*
Capers
Anchovies
Flour *(plain and self raising - sometimes known as 'cake' flour)*
Rice *(arborio and long grain)*
Dry pasta *(spaghetti and short pasta - e.g. penne, rigatoni)*
Semolina *(can buy from health food section)*
Polenta
Parmesan Cheese *(no, not the stuff in the cardboard tube!)*
Dried herbs *(oregano, bay leaves, thyme)*
Eggs
Sugar

cooking tips from the italian kitchen

Ask a group of people to name an Italian dish and it is guaranteed some will say pasta, some will say pizza, and others will say risotto. To prepare these well you will benefit from getting your head around the following ...

OLIVE OIL

Here is my rough guide to the different types of olive oil and their uses. Don't get too hung up though; like most things in Italy there is no one-size-fits-all rule.

Extra Virgin - comes from the first cold pressing and is considered the best type of olive oil. However cooking with it over heat destroys the flavour because at 42 degrees Celsius the vitamin content changes and the enzymes are destroyed. It's best used as a dip for breads or to drizzle over dishes before serving

Virgin - comes from the first pressing of mature olives. Generally also avoid using it for cooking and primarily use it for dressings and marinades

Olive Oil - mostly comes from the second pressing. It can handle high heat and is therefore good for cooking and frying

Light Olive Oil - whilst London-based Italian chef and restaurateur, Giorgio Locatelli, insists on avoiding this at all cost, it does have its limited uses, such as cooking at high temperatures or frying when you don't want a strong olive oil flavour

PASTA

Forget the urban myth that Marco Polo introduced spaghetti to Italy upon returning from a visit to China. The Romans ate the first pasta eaten in Italy, made from hard durum wheat and called Laganum.

Pasta is essentially the vehicle for best transporting a particular type of sauce to your mouth. This marriage between pasta and sauce makes it essential you choose the right sauce for the particular type of pasta you are cooking. There are no fixed rules but traditional dishes offer some guidelines:

- Sauces that cling, such as those made with eggs, cream, grated cheese, olive oil, butter, and herbs, are ideal with long thin pasta such as fettuccine, tagliatelle and spaghetti.

- Chunky sauces go well with pasta shapes that can hold them, like tiny cups, such as orecchiette and rotelle, or are hollow, such as penne and rigatoni.

Basic Steps to cooking Pasta Al Dente

Al Dente - this literally means 'on the tooth' but its essence means to be cooked so as to be firm when eaten. The phrase 'al dente' comes into play as the best way to test if the pasta is ready is to fish out a small piece and bite it between your front teeth.

Step 1 - Bring a large pot of water to the boil.
Use one litre (2.1 pts) of water for every 100g (3.5 oz) of pasta; giving the pasta room to move is crucial, otherwise it runs the risk of becoming gluey. It also accommodates the release of significant amounts of starch.

Step 2 - Once it is boiling, add a couple of pinches of salt, add the pasta, and bring the water back to the boil.
It's a myth that you need to add olive oil to prevent the pasta sticking (it actually stops the sauce clinging to the pasta when you serve it). Simply try to let the pasta fall gently out of your hands into the water rather than feeding it in clumps.

Put the lid on the pan immediately to bring the water back to the boil in the shortest time. As soon as it has reached boiling point again, remove the lid and loosen the pasta.

Start timing as soon as the water comes back to the boil. Start testing on the teeth about two minutes before you think it should be ready.

Step 3 - Drain the pasta into a colander in a sink.
Don't drain the pasta too thoroughly or it will dry out. Instead either throw it immediately back into the pot the second it has hit the colander (this requires a little dexterity), or reserve a little of the cooking water.

PIZZA

Whilst every Italian family has its own version of pizza dough, here is the simplest and most idiot-proof method I have found.

Ingredients to make approx. 8 thin pizza bases
(20cm (8 inch) diameter each)

- 1 kg (2.2 lbs) plain flour
- Dry yeast (powder) - 1% of the weight of the flour
- Salt - 1% of the weight of the flour
- Water - approx. 1 litre (2.1 pts) for every kilogram (2.2 lbs) of flour used
- Extra flour for dusting

Step 1 - Combine the flour and the salt in a large bowl. Mix it thoroughly with your fingers so as to work the salt evenly through the flour. The main reason for this is that should the yeast, when added, come into direct contact with the salt it will likely die (yes, yeast can be killed) and therefore not activate the rising process.

Step 2 - Sprinkle the yeast over the flour and work through with your fingers.

Step 3 - Add half the water and work through the flour mixture. Continue to add small amounts of water and work through. (*Italian Secret: The exact amount of water required will vary from* *one batch to the next. It's easier to be conservative and add more water as you need it than it is to take water away!)*

Step 4 - Once the mixture has come together as one blob, lightly flour a bench and dump the blob onto the bench and begin to knead for approximately 8 - 10 minutes until the dough has a smooth shiny texture.

Step 5 - Put the dough back in your bowl, cover with a couple of towels in order to create a warm and draught-free environment for between 1.5 - 2 hours (essentially until it has about doubled in size; this will take longer in winter than summer).

Step 6 - Lightly flour your bench again and break off a piece of dough about one-and-a-half times the size of your fist. Work this into a ball and place on the bench. Repeat this until you have used all the dough and then cover them with the towels for another 30 minutes (they will again nearly double in size)

Step 7 - Lightly oil your pizza trays and, using your fingers, spread the dough to the perimeter of the trays.

You are now ready to add your topping and cook them!

One point to note regarding the 'right' type of flour to use. Some books insist you use doppio zero ('00') flour, though Luisa's grandmother just uses supermarket brand plain flour with spectacular results.

RISOTTO

I have a 'contentious' Italian secret - risotto should never be stirred. When you stir, you make the risotto gluggy. Instead, it should look wet and you should see every grain. I say this secret is contentious because my mother-in-law thinks it's a ridiculous notion and my father-in-law has nothing against gluggy risotto! I am not going to force this issue - I think it is great either way. One

VITAL thing to note - if you are going to try the no-stir approach ENSURE you use a non-stick pan.

Tips:
1. Ensure the stock is good quality, as the dish is composed of 50 - 60% stock.
2. The stock should be just below boiling as it is added to the rice, otherwise it will drop the temperature of the risotto.
3. Add the stock slowly so the rice stays wet, though not drowning, before adding another ladle.
4. Use a wide, heavy-bottomed pot on a medium heat - too hot and the rice will stick to the pan; too cold and it will cook unevenly.
5. Just before you take the risotto off the heat, add a ladle full of stock. The Venetians call this all'onda, which means 'on the wave' - this loosens the risotto just before you serve it.

a few recipes of summer

PESTO

Pesto is a somewhat addictive condiment that Luisa has vowed she could survive on, if given the choice. Having eaten it last year in Genoa, where it was invented, Luisa would agree with the statement, "Once you've eaten a good pesto in Genoa, it's easy to forget that any other dishes exist."[42] You can spread it on bread or crackers, use it as a dip, stir it through freshly cooked spaghetti, add it to soup at the time of serving (esp. minestrone).

2 garlic cloves
50g (1.5 oz) pine nuts
80g (3 oz) basil leaves
2 tablespoons grated parmesan cheese
2 tablespoons grated pecorino cheese
150ml (4.8 fl oz) extra virgin olive oil

Put the garlic, pine nuts, basil and cheese in a mortar and pestle or a food processor and pound to mix to a paste. Add the oil in a steady stream, mixing constantly. Add salt if necessary. Refrigerate in a sterilised jar, covered with a layer of olive oil for up to three weeks.

Italian Secret = *Many recipes simply use parmesan cheese, which tastes good in this dish, however believe me when I say that the salty pecorino takes this dish to new heights. We first had this half-parmesan/half-pecorino combination when we were in Genoa (the home of pesto) and there is no turning back!*

IBM Secret = *Pine nuts are ridiculously expensive, which can be a turn-off to making pesto. Additionally, fresh pine nuts are not always easy to come by (i.e. they are normally only found in growers' markets and the like) and you have to settle for the ones in packets next to the spice section of the supermarket. Therefore a number of Australians are marketing pesto made with almonds. Try regular almonds (the fresher the better) or even roasted almonds for a different flavour.*

TOMATO AND BASIL BRUSCHETTA

This will take you less than ten minutes to pull together. If you are ever stuck for a quick and simple lunch idea on a lazy weekend ... this is the answer. Also hits the spot on a summer's evening when you come home from work and can't be bothered slaving in the kitchen.

4 large slices of crusty Italian bread
1 garlic clove, sliced in half
6 tomatoes
6 basil leaves, roughly torn
Extra virgin olive oil
Drizzle of extra virgin olive oil

Roughly chop the tomatoes and mix with the basil. Season with salt and pepper. Mix through about two tablespoons of extra virgin olive oil.

Grill or toast the bread until it is crisp. Cut the garlic clove in half and rub the cut edge over both sides of each bread slice. Drizzle a little olive oil over each bread slice.

Pile the tomato and basil mix onto each slice of bruschetta.

APRICOT JAM
Marmellata di Albicocche

I was inspired to start making my own jam when I struggled to find 'jam' on the supermarket shelves. I could only locate 'preserve' (which is meant to indicate it is mainly made from fruit), 'conserve' (slightly less fruit than 'preserve') and 'jelly' (more juice, concentrate, additives and chemicals than fruit). I take great heart in knowing what goes into my homemade jam ... that is 'fruit'!

1.2 kg (2.6 lbs). ripe apricots
Grated zest of 1 small lemon
250 ml (8 fl oz). water
550 g (1.2 lbs). caster sugar

Wash the apricots, cut them into pieces and discard the pips. Put them into a saucepan with the lemon zest and water, and bring to the boil. Cook for about 15 minutes on a medium heat to soften. Add the sugar and continue cooking on a low heat for another hour, stirring frequently to prevent it from sticking.

Remove from the heat.

Pour the hot jam into clean, sterilised jars and close the lids tightly. Put the jars upright into a large saucepan, cover with cold water and bring to the boil. Boil for 20 minutes, remove from the heat and leave the jars to cool in the water before removing them. Check the lids to ensure that a vacuum has been created.

Italian Secret = *Line the bottom of your saucepan with tea towels to prevent the jars bouncing around and place a tea towel on the top to help prevent the water boiling over.*

Store upright in a cool dark place. The jam will keep for up to a year.

a few recipes of autumn

BAKED EGGPLANT WITH TOMATO, MOZZARELLA AND PARMESAN CHEESE

Melanzane alla Parmigiana

Every Italian family has its own version of this dish. I have a 100% success rate in converting people who profess not to like eggplant, by serving them this dish.

3 medium eggplants, cut into 3 mm (0.1 inch) slices
2 tablespoons. olive oil
2 garlic cloves, peeled and finely chopped
5 tomatoes, skinned and chopped (or 400 g (15 oz). tin of peeled tomatoes, chopped)
10 basil leaves, roughly torn
Flour
Olive oil
300g (10 oz). fresh mozzarella cheese, cut into 5 mm (0.2 inch) slices
50g (1.5 oz). freshly grated parmesan cheese

Cut the eggplant into slices and put them in a colander. Sprinkle with salt and leave for about 30 minutes to allow the bitter juices to drain away. (Italian Secret = The larger the eggplant, the longer you will have to leave it 'under salt')

Preheat the oven to 180° C (350° F)

To make the tomato sauce, heat the 2 tablespoons of olive oil in a saucepan. Add the garlic and soften. Add the tomatoes and half of the basil. Season with salt and pepper, and simmer for 15-20 minutes, or until the tomatoes have melted into a sauce.

Rinse the eggplant slices and pat dry with paper towels. Lightly dust both sides with flour. Heat enough olive oil to come 1 cm (0.4 inch) up the side of a saucepan. Heat the oil and fry the eggplants in batches until golden brown on both sides, adding more oil as needed. Transfer them to a plate lined with paper towels to absorb the oil.

Spoon a little of the tomato sauce into a greased 32 x 20cm (12 x 8.5 inch) oven dish. Cover with a layer of eggplant slices, slightly overlapping one another. Season with pepper.

Add a few spoonfuls of tomato sauce, then a layer of the mozzarella cheese slices. Add the remaining basil leaves. Sprinkle with Parmesan cheese. Repeat to use up the ingredients. Put into the hot oven and bake for 30 minutes or until the top is lightly golden and crusty. Cool slightly before cutting into servings.

BISTECCA ALLA PIZZAIOLA

As with so many dishes in which tomatoes are a strong component, and like Luisa, this dish hails from Napoli.

4 steaks
4 tablespoons olive oil
560g (1.2 lbs) tomatoes (or equivalent size can of peeled and chopped tomatoes)
3 garlic cloves, crushed
3 basil leaves, torn into pieces
1 teaspoon finely chopped parsley
Salt
Pepper

Season the steaks with salt and pepper. Put on a plate and set aside.

Score a cross in the top of each tomato. Plunge into boiling water for 20 seconds, then drain and peel the skin away from the cross. Chop the tomatoes, discarding the cores.

Heat 2 tablespoons of the olive oil in a saucepan over low heat and add the garlic. Soften without browning for 1-2 minutes, then add the tomato and season. Increase the heat, bring to the boil and cook for 5 minutes. Stir in the basil.

Heat the remaining oil in a frying pan with a tight-fitting lid. Brown the steaks over moderately high heat for 2 minutes on each side. Place in a slightly overlapping row down the centre of the pan and spoon the sauce over the top, covering the steaks completely. Cover the pan and cook over low heat for about 5 minutes, or until the steaks are cooked to your taste. Sprinkle the parsley over the top and serve.

PIZZA MARGHERITA

With its red, white and green colours (the colours of the Italian flag), this classic was first created in 1889 by Raffaele Eposito in honour of Queen Margherita, who had heard so much of the fabled pizzas of Naples that she requested one to eat when she visited the city.

1 x 20 - 30cm (8 - 12 inch) pizza base
1/2 cup tomato sauce
150g (5 oz) mozzarella, sliced
9 basil leaves
1 tablespoon olive oil
Cornmeal

Preheat the oven to 240°C (460° F). Place the pizza base on a tray dusted with cornmeal, and spoon the tomato sauce, spreading it up to the rim. Scatter with the mozzarella and basil and drizzle with the oil.

Bake for 12-15 minutes or until golden. Remove from the oven and brush the rim with a little extra olive oil before serving to make the crust crunchy and golden.

*(**Italian Secrets**: Take the pizza out about half-way through cooking and put the mozzarella on at this time ... it will reduce the likelihood of the cheese burning and therefore keep it a little moist; Additionally, scatter the basil on at the end of the cooking process - again this will prevent it from burning and the heat from the cooked pizza will cause the leaves to wilt down nicely)*

a few recipes of winter

SPAGHETTI WITH GARLIC, OLIVE OIL AND CHILLI

Spaghetti Aglio, Olio E Peperoncino

Luisa's Dad (and his friends) traditionally have their wives cook this quick and simple meal when they return home from an Italian wedding reception where they considered the food to have been of an inadequate quantity and/or quality. I tend to cook this after a Sunday night at Church. The only question this dish leaves you with is the classic conundrum 'can-you-ever-have-too-much-garlic'?

500g (1.1 lb) Spaghetti (Serves 4 people)
125 ml (4.16 fl oz) extra virgin olive oil
3 small dried red chilies
3 garlic cloves, peeled and finely chopped
Small handful chopped fresh parsley
Grated Parmesan cheese (Try to avoid using the stuff in cardboard tubes, which I suspect is made from the very cardboard it is stored in!)

This is a quick, simple sauce, ready in the time that it takes to cook the spaghetti. You can add more or less garlic and chili to suit your taste.

Put a large saucepan of salted water to the boil on the stove.

When it comes to the boil, add the pasta and cook.

Put the olive oil, chili and garlic into a saucepan large enough to hold all the pasta. Heat until the garlic and chili begin to sizzle, and colour and flavour the oil. (**Italian Secret** = *Add the garlic at* the beginning, before you heat the oil, as this will prevent it burning) Remove the saucepan from the heat.

Drain the pasta. Add the pasta to the oil with the parsley, tossing quickly to coat all of the pasta strands. Serve immediately with Parmesan cheese and an extra drizzle of olive oil.

MINESTRONE ALLA GENOVESE

Mixed Vegetable Soup - Genoa Style

Some minestrone recipes don't have the pancetta, however buy the one crusted in chili flakes as it adds a nice hint of heat to the finished soup. Also, the addition of the pesto is the thing that takes this from 'regular' minestrone to 'alla Genovese' - it's not vital, however it too takes the finished dish to a new level. As for the choice of vegetables, there are not too many hard and fast rules - this soup gives you the flexibility to vary them according to the season.

220 g (8 oz) borlotti beans, drained
50 g (1.5 oz) butter
1 large onion, finely chopped
1 garlic clove, finely chopped
15 g (0.5 oz) parsley, finely chopped
2 sage leaves
100 g (3.5 oz) pancetta, cubed (i.e. not slices of pancetta, but the blocks)
2 celery stalks, halved then sliced
2 carrots, sliced
3 potatoes, peeled but left whole
1 teaspoon tomato puree
400 g (15 oz) tin chopped tomatoes
8 basil leaves
3 litres (6.3 pts) chicken or vegetable stock
2 courgettes, sliced
220 g (0.5 lbs) shelled peas
120 g (4 oz) runner beans, cut into 4 cm (1.6 inch) lengths

1/4 cabbage, shredded
150 g (5 oz) soup (small) pasta
3 tablespoons pesto
Parmesan cheese, grated

Melt the butter in a large saucepan and add the onion, garlic, parsley, sage and pancetta. Cook over low heat, stirring once or twice, for about 10 minutes, or until the onion is soft and golden.

Add the celery, carrot and potatoes and cook for 5 minutes. Stir in the tomato puree, tomatoes, basil and borlotti beans. Season with plenty of pepper. Add the stock and bring slowly to the boil. Cover and leave to simmer for 2 hours, stirring once or twice.

If the potatoes haven't already broken up, roughly break them up with a fork against the side of the pan. Taste for seasoning and add the courgettes, peas, runner beans, cabbage and pasta. Simmer until the pasta is al dente. Serve with a dollop of pesto and the Parmesan.

CHICKEN CACCIATORA

Hunter's Style Chicken

I would have to say this is one of my favourite winter meals - hearty and tender, guaranteed to warm you and satisfy you from the inside out.

3 tablespoons olive oil
1 large onion, finely chopped
3 garlic cloves, crushed
1 stalk celery, finely chopped
150 g (5 oz) pancetta, finely chopped
125 g (4.5 oz) button mushrooms, thickly sliced
4 chicken drumsticks
4 chicken thighs
90 ml (3.2 fl oz) dry red or white wine
2 x 400 g (15 oz) tins chopped tomatoes
1/4 teaspoon of brown sugar
1 oregano sprig, plus 4-5 sprigs to garnish
1 rosemary sprig
1 bay leaf

Heat half the oil in large heavy based saucepan. Add the onion, garlic and celery and cook, stirring from time to time, over moderately low heat for 6-8 minutes until the onion is golden

Add the pancetta and mushrooms, increase the heat and cook, stirring occasionally, for 5 minutes. Spoon out onto a plate and set aside.

Add the remaining olive oil to the pan and lightly brown the chicken pieces, a few at a time. Season them as they brown. Spoon off any excess fat and return all the pieces to the casserole. Add the wine, increase the heat and cook until the liquid has almost evaporated.

Add the tomatoes, sugar, oregano, rosemary, bay leaf and 75 ml (2.4 fl oz) cold water. Bring to the boil then stir in the reserved pancetta mixture. Cover and leave to simmer for 20 minutes, or until the chicken is tender but not falling off the bone.

If the liquid is too thin, remove the chicken from the pan, increase the heat and boil until thickened. Discard the sprigs of herbs and taste for salt and pepper. Toss in the additional oregano sprigs and the dish is ready to serve.

a few recipes of spring

CHARGRILLED ASPARAGUS

Every year I look forward to Spring, if only for fresh, inexpensive asparagus. Once you learn a couple of simple must-do's, like how to snap off the woody ends, it is an easy, tasty and rather versatile vegetable.

24 asparagus spears
1 tablespoon extra virgin olive oil
2 tablespoons balsamic vinegar
Parmesan shavings

Wash the asparagus and remove the woody ends (hold each spear at both ends and bend it gently - it will snap at its natural breaking point).

Put the asparagus in a bowl, add the olive oil and toss well. Heat a griddle or barbecue (you can use a large diameter frypan) and cook the asparagus for about 10 minutes, or until al dente. Drizzle with balsamic vinegar and sprinkle with the Parmesan to serve.

RISOTTO AGLI ASPARAGI

Asparagus Risotto

Many people think of risotto as being a white dish, however that does not have to be the case. Saffron risotto turns out a lovely orange/yellow and this dish an interesting green! I have seen a recipe for Asparagus Risotto that uses saffron, though not having tried it I can only guess it comes out a nice light green.

1 kg (2.2 lbs) asparagus
500 ml (1 pt) chicken stock
500 ml (1 pt) vegetable stock
4 tablespoons olive oil
1 small onion, finely chopped (you could use a couple of French shallots instead)
350 g (13 oz) risotto rice
75 g (2.5 oz) Parmesan, grated
3 tablespoons double cream

Wash the asparagus and remove the woody ends. Cook the asparagus stems in boiling water until tender (about 8 minutes). Drain and place in a blender with the chicken and vegetable stocks (You can use just one type of stock if you wish). Blend for 1 minute, then put in a saucepan, bring to the boil and maintain at a low simmer.

Cook the asparagus tips in boiling water for 1 minute, drain and refresh in iced water.

Heat the olive oil in a large wide heavy-based saucepan. Add the onion and cook until softened. Add the rice and reduce the heat to low. Season and stir briefly to thoroughly coat the rice. Stir in a ladleful of the simmering stock and cook over moderate heat, stirring continuously (unless you want to bow to my 'Contentious Italian Secret'). When the stock has been absorbed, stir in another ladleful. Continue like this for about twenty minutes, until all the stock has been added and the rice is al dente. (Whatever you do - don't rush this part of the process. I ensure I have a little spuntino to nibble on while I am cooking this to help my patience)

Add the parmesan and cream and gently stir in the asparagus tips. Season with salt and pepper and serve hot.

FRIED, CRUMBED LAMB CUTLETS

Cotolette di Agnello Fritte

This method of preparation will make even the toughest of meat tender. It also allows you to 'stretch' how far your meat goes. You can also prepare chicken breasts this way. For example, if you buy thick chicken breasts and cook them you will find it difficult to cook them evenly and thoroughly. Simply cut them in half horizontally and then prepare them as below ... beautiful!

5 eggs
240 g (3 cups) breadcrumbs
18 medium-sized lamb chops, trimmed of fat
Light olive oil for shallow frying
Lemon wedges, to serve

Whip the eggs in a wide bowl and season with salt and pepper. Put the breadcrumbs on a large flat plate. Flatten the chops with a meat mallet and dip them into the egg to cover completely. Shake off the excess and pat them into the breadcrumbs on both sides, pressing down with your palm to ensure they stick. Transfer them to a large clean plate until you are ready to fry them

Pour enough oil into a deep frypan to ensure the chops can be shallow-fried without sticking to the bottom. Heat the oil on a medium-low heat, and when it is hot, begin frying the cutlets in batches. Fry on both sides until they are golden brown, crispy and cooked through.

Transfer the cooked cutlets to a plate lined with paper towels to absorb the excess oil while you finish frying the rest. Pile them up onto a clean platter, sprinkle with salt and serve the cutlets with lemon wedges.

salvation prayer

In the title of this book I have used the expression 'Church Family'. You may have picked up this book and wondered if that meant you. Well, I am happy to let you know that anybody can be part of the global 'Church Family'. The 'Church Family' is made up of over two billion people who have committed their lives to following Jesus Christ.

My prayer for you is that you would come to know Jesus Christ as your friend and Saviour and, in doing so, become part of the 'Church Family'.

Committing to following Jesus is as simple and powerful as sincerely praying a prayer. If you are not sure that you know God, and that you are going to Heaven, then make this your prayer today ...

'Dear Lord Jesus

I come to You today and confess that I need You ...
Please come into my heart ... Jesus ... be my Lord and Saviour ...
Wash me ... Cleanse me ... and forgive me all of my sins ...

Thank you for giving me a brand new start ...
Today I open my life to You ... I am now a child of the King ...

Amen'

Where To From Here?

If you just prayed that prayer then write or e-mail me and I will send you a little booklet called 'The Journey', written by my good friend Phil Baker, which gives you some great starting points.

Being connected into a great Church is vital in your ongoing Christian journey. If you are not connected into a Church please let me know, as we know many great Churches in most countries around the world and would love to help you get connected.

Mark Pomery

about the author

Mark Pomery is one of Australia's leading young communicators. Mark speaks in churches, conferences, and business meetings throughout Australia and internationally, delivering messages designed specifically to cause the listeners to expand in every area of their lives.

Since 1997 Mark has been a Minister at Riverview Church in Perth, Western Australia, a contemporary church which attracts around 4000 people each weekend.

Mark is currently the Director of International Development for Riverview Church and its various ministry initiatives, including the 500Plus Church Network, the Building Business Leaders Network, and the New Church Network.

For more information about Mark, including his itinerary, additional resources, and more Italian By Marriage stuff, visit

www.markpomery.com

"I would love to stay in touch with you as our journeys continue to unfold. Go to my website and send me your details through the Contact page."
- Marco

endnotes & design bits

endnotes

1.   *King Lear*, William Shakespeare
2.   Matthew Chapter 10, Verse 8 *(New International Version)*
3.   Philippians 4: 10 - 13 *(New International Version)*
4.   Malachi Chapter 3 Verse 10b *(New International Version)*
5.   Proverbs Chapter 29 Verse 19 *(King James Version)*
6.   Proverbs Chapter 11, Verse 24 *(The Message)*
7.   Matthew Chapter 5, Verse 16 *(The Message)*
8.   Acts Chapter 4 Verse 32 *(New International Version)*
9.   *"It's All Italiano To Me"*; (www.franklotito.com.au)
10.   'Shed-o' is 'Dinglish' (a strange and wonderful language created by the Italian immigrants to Australia which blends Italian and English) for shed ... Italian-Australians have at least two in their backyards!
11.   This statement struggled to pass the proof readers - I had to assure them this is exactly how she says it.
12.   2 Thessalonians Chapter 3 Verse 10 *(New International Version)*
13.   *Candide*, 1759 Penguin Classics; Reissue edition (June 30, 1950)
14.   *Speech at The New York State Fair*, 7 September 1903
15.   Proverbs Chapter 13, Verse 4 *(New Living Translation)*
16.   Colossians Chapter 3, Verse 23 *(New Living Translation)*
17.   Robert Frost, *'Mountain Interval'* 1920; Collectors Reprints Inc. 1995
18.   2 Thessalonians 3: 11 - 13 *(New International Version)*
19.   1 Timothy 1: 18; 1 Timothy 6: 12 *(New International Version)*
20.   Matthew 11: 12 *(New International Version)*
21.   *www.usatoday.com* 18th December 2005
22.   Matthew Chapter 10, Verse 39 *(New International Version)*
23.   Acts 2: 44 - 45; *(New International Version)*
24.   Ephesians Chapter 4, Verses 15-16 *(New International Version)*
25.   Matthew Chapter 11, Verse 12 *(New International Version)*
26.   Matthew Chapter 6, Verse 12 *(New International Version)*

27. Paul Hoffman 'That Fine Italian Hand' p.45; Holt (Henry) & Co ,U.S. 1991

28. Nikko Amandonico 'La Pizza - The True Story From Naples' p.12; Mitchell Beazley, May 2001

29. Paul Hoffman 'That Fine Italian Hand' p.108; Holt (Henry) & Co ,U.S. 1991

30. Christopher Duggan 'A Concise History Of Italy' p.31 Cambridge University Press, April 1994

31. Proverbs Chapter 29, Verse 18 (New American Standard Version)

32. Deuteronomy Chapter 8 Verse 18 (New International Version)

33. Tim Parks 'An Italian Education' pp 142 - 143; Vintage, May 2001

34. Andrea de Jorio 'Gestures In Naples And Gesture In Classical Antiquity' p.cii; Indiana University Press; Reprint edition, January 2002

35. Ibid

36. Ibid

37. Matthew Fort 'Eating Up Italy' Perennial, May 2004

38. New International Version

39. John Chapter 10 Verse 10 (The Message)

40. Robert Browning Prospice; As published in 'The Major Works'; Oxford University Press, December 2005

41. Galatians Chapter 6 Verse 9 (New International Version)

42. Barbara Hodgson, Italy Out Of Hand; Chronicle Books, May 2005

design notes

about the font

"Eric Gill was a versatile and brilliant talent. He was active, prolific and successful in many disciplines from wood engraving to sculpture and calligraphy. In the 1920s he turned his creativity to type design and, in 1928, Gill Sans was born. Gill spent much of the 1930s further developing the Gill Sans family and the result is one of his most successful and widely used typeface designs

One of reasons for the enduring success of Gill Sans is that it is based on Roman character shapes and proportions and is unlike virtually any other sans serif typeface. There is a warmth and humanity found in the face that is found in few sans serif designs. Each weight also retains a distinct character of its own. They were not "mechanically" produced from a single design, as is the case with many other sans serif designs. The Light, with its heavily kerned 'f' and tall 't,' is open and elegant. The Regular, with its flat-bottomed 'd,' flat-topped 'p' and 'q,' and triangular-topped 't' has a more compact and muscular appearance. The **Bold** tends to echo the softer, more open style of the Light, while the **Extra Bold** and **Ultra Bold** have their own vivid personalities.

While they have different personalities, all the fonts of the Gill Sans family also work in perfect harmony. Whether on a single page or in long document, Gill Sans quietly unifies any graphic content.

Gill's approach to type design was uniform, consistent and appropriate. His goals were to create, "Absolutely legible-to-the-last-degree letters, provide beauty of form to all printed communication, and to maintain the dignity of hand drawn letterforms." Eric Gill's talent, skill and craftsman ethos are perfectly reflected in the Gill Sans family."

as quoted from the website www.fonts.com

photography

Photos used are from the authors private collection with the exception of those listed below.

p12. ©photographer: Raymond Lampard
p146. ©photographer: Belinda McCullough
p150. ©photographer: Lisa McDonald | Agency: Dreamstime.com
p160. ©photographer: Cheng-jih Chen | Agency: Dreamstime.com
p166. image provided by Dreamstime.com
p172. image provided by Dreamstime.com
p180. ©photographer: Stephen Snyder | Agency: Dreamstime.com
p192. ©photographer: Gaylene Trethewey
photo of author on backcover ©photographer: Gaylene Trethewey

cartoons

Italian Family used on front cover and map of Italy used on last page ©cartoonist: Rod Jefferson

artwork & design

by Belinda McCullough of BAM Graphic Design
email: bamdesigns@westnet.com.au